DICTIONARY
OF
AQUARIUM
TERMS

D0730510

John H. Tullock

DICTIONARY
OF
AQUARIUM TERMS

Dictionary Illustrations by Virge Kask
Anatomical Illustrations by Michele Earle-Bridges
With Full-color Photographs by Aarron Norman

BARRON'S

© Copyright 2000 by Barron's Educational Series, Inc.

Dictionary Illustrations © Copyright 2000 by Virge Kask

All rights reserved.

No part of this book may be reproduced in any form, by photostat, microfilm, xerography, or any other means, or incorporated into any information retrieval system, electronic or mechanical, without the written permission of the copyright owner.

All inquiries should be addressed to:
Barron's Educational Series, Inc.
250 Wireless Boulevard
Hauppauge, New York 11788
http://www.barronseduc.com

International Standard Book No. 0-7641-1165-5

Library of Congress Catalog Card No. 99-46592

Library of Congress Cataloging-in-Publication Data

Tullock, John H., 1951–
    Dictionary of aquarium terms / John H. Tullock;
    illustrations by Virge Kask. p. cm.
    Includes bibliographical references (p.).
    ISBN 0-7641-1165-5 (alk. paper)
    1. Aquariums—Dictionaries. 2. Marine aquariums—Dictionaries.
    3. Aquarium animals—Dictionaries. 4. Marine aquarium ani-
    mals—Dictionaries. I. Title.

SF457.3 .T85   2000
639.34'03—dc21   99-46592

Printed in the United States of America

9 8 7 6 5 4 3 2 1

CONTENTS

INTRODUCTION

The Allure of the Aquarium

Human beings have been keeping fish and other aquatic creatures in enclosures for thousands of years. Ancient cultures probably first kept sea creatures alive in captivity in order to have fresh seafood available. Accounts of such "aquariums" date back to ancient Egypt. In Rome, fish-holding tubs called *piscinae* have been found in the gardens of the wealthy and powerful. In the New World, containers for freshwater and marine fish adorned Montezuma's gardens. In China, fishkeeping dates to the tenth century. The Chinese cultivated certain fish, such as goldfish, solely for their ornamental value. Metal-framed, ornately ornamented glass boxes holding displays of plants, fish, and invertebrates from exotic locales that we recognize as aquariums first appeared in the Victorian era. The modern aquarium, one that attempts to create the illusion of a window revealing a glimpse of the underwater world, is a relatively recent phenomenon.

The biggest problems facing early aquarists were an inadequate understanding of ecology and a lack of suitable technological aids, most of which were developed after the advent of electricity, to foster and maintain ecological processes essential to the stability of the captive environment. They did recognize, however, that the plants and animals confined to the aquarium were mutually dependent. The aquariums they built attempted to achieve an often elusive "balance" between respiration and photosynthesis that would permit the system to operate over a long period of time. This type of system, in which plants, gravel, sand, rocks, and fish were essentially scooped up from a native stream and placed into a glass box, the plants being relied upon to absorb wastes and to release oxygen for the benefit of the fish, remained the typical aquarium design in both home and laboratory until after World War II. By the 1950s such gadgets as small-scale air pumps and immersion heaters made keeping tropical fish and plants a possibility for almost anyone. Virtually all of the hobby aquariums in existence exhibited freshwater species. With the advent of home marine aquariums in the 1960s, coupled with the still-continuing construction of large public aquariums in the world's major cities, the aquarium hobby has undergone significant changes.

The Saltwater Aquarium in the Home was a popular little book written in 1959 by the late Robert Straughan. It was the first attempt to offer suggestions for maintaining a marine aquarium to hobbyists in the United States. In the early days of marine aquariums, big, boldly colored fish from halfway around the world practically sold themselves. Dealers sold what collectors shipped to them, and fish were housed in aquariums fitted with undergravel filters and decorated with dead coral skeletons. Hobbyists purchased what was available for sale. On only the rarest occasions would an interesting little fish, a strange invertebrate, or a piece of living seaweed find its way into a shop.

Marine aquarium keeping has experienced expanded horizons over the last two decades. Life forms available to aquarists now come from a variety of geographic locations, and an even wider variety of microhabitats. New understanding of marine ecology and the life habits of a broad range of species make maintenance of appropriate conditions less hit or miss. The changing nature of the aquarium business, from sideline to front line, wrought by the developing interest in marine aquarium keeping, led to widespread changes throughout other branches of the aquarium hobby. "Old-fashioned" freshwater tanks with luxuriant growths of living aquatic plants, made easier and more reliable with the advent of modern devices like high-intensity lighting, enjoyed a comeback that continues unabated. Similarly, keeping communities of the rock-dwelling cichlids of the rift lakes of eastern Africa has been facilitated by more efficient filtration systems and better understanding of the ecology of these species. Aquariums have also become more fashionable in recent years. Although trendsetters once considered them either educational toys or a pastime suitable only for slightly daffy maiden aunts or eccentric, academic types, aquariums now adorn luxury hotels, cruise ships, and the homes of the rich and famous.

Overlain upon the past four decades of change within the aquarium hobby itself is the change in public attitudes regarding the ecosystems that nurture Earth's life forms. Aquariums both public and private have become more than underwater menageries. Both are recognized as impressively powerful research tools and as cradles of hope for the survival of many unusual and obscure species whose future in the wild appears bleak. Further, the aquarium industry provides income for developing countries from which many species are collected. Perhaps it was inevitable that interested amateurs and seasoned professional scientists would share their knowledge and work together for the protection of aquatic species, but the alliance between aquarium keeping and conservation has been long in coming. Where it has taken root, however, such cooperation has already begun to bear fruit.

Because of new capabilities, new understanding and the availability of an ever-widening range of species, aquariums have evolved far beyond mere displays of fish. Aquarists are recreating in the aquarium a tiny segment of a specific biotope, complete with a cross section of appropriate, diverse life forms.

In short, aquarium keeping has come of age. The modern aquarist must be engineer, ecologist, artist, and handyman in order to create and maintain aquariums that not only reflect nature but provide the best possible life support system for their inhabitants. Wearing each of these hats requires familiarity with a polyglot of specialized terminology, some unique to the aquarium world, and some borrowed from a host of technical disciplines.

This book is an effort to promote a common language among all people with an interest in aquarium keeping. It is intended to dispel mystery for the beginning hobbyist and to help bring clarity to the vast literature reporting on the work of dedicated aquarists—amateur and professional—worldwide. Inevitably, this first attempt at a modern aquarium dictionary will create controversy, although that is not the author's purpose or intent. Reader input is actively solicited for improving the content, including additional terms, and identifying and correcting errors.

In particular, some will find fault in the handling of the taxonomic information. The literature concerning the classification and evolutionary biology of fish alone is imponderably vast, never mind that relating to aquatic invertebrates and plants. Further, the existence of ongoing research virtually guarantees that taxonomic data, in particular the assignment of species to genera and families, will change with time. While every attempt has been made to reflect the most recent taxonomic information, some generic names and their definitions will no doubt be considered invalid by experts. In cases where generic names that are now considered invalid are nevertheless still used extensively within the aquarium industry or in a large body of existing aquarium literature, I have included the old name, with an appropriate explanation. This was done to facilitate making connections between old and new works. Many older books and magazine articles are still of great value to those now trying to maintain or breed certain species. The fish, of course, do not change; however, both scientific names and the opinions of taxonomists do.

Another consideration has been the organization and presentation of the taxonomic information. To facilitate the reader's ability to quickly locate specific facts, the author has abandoned the almost universal practice of including a hierarchical classification scheme (destined for future revisions, in any case) in favor of simply including the generic names for aquarium organisms along with the alphabetic listings of other terms. To include in this book every group of organisms that has, or might be, displayed in an aquarium would be cumbersome and serve no good purpose. The taxonomic references chosen for inclusion are genus names for the majority of organisms regularly available in the aquarium hobby trade. In defining each genus, the author has avoided repetitive phrases such as "a genus of" or "a species of" in the listings. Readers should take note, however, that in most cases the listed genus is not the only example of its family to be found in nature. Readers interested in a more detailed consideration of the evolutionary relationships among species and higher taxa may wish to consult references suggested in the Selected Bibliography (see page 197).

Terms have been defined as they are employed in the aquarium industry or hobby, rather than with strict regard to the area of knowledge to which the term refers. What I have attempted to do is to create a definition that would be considered correct by an expert in the appropriate field, but not necessarily a definition that would be all-encompassing. Thus, an ichthyologist might employ a somewhat different definition of "pectoral fin" from the one found here, but an accountant using this dictionary should be able to locate the pectoral fins on his pet oscar without difficulty.

From elaborate decorations for posh hotel lobbies to artificial refuges for endangered species, aquariums exist in all sizes and for a multiplicity of uses, bringing the natural world into the home, enabling otherwise unaffordable or impossible scientific research, educating both children and adults, cultivating an assortment of aquatic organisms for food, medicine, and ornament, providing wholesome family entertainment, reducing anxiety, and lowering blood pressure. Technology now reaches far beyond the Roman *piscina*, but the allure of the aquarium remains, as always, the opportunity to look within a world of which we humans can never really be a part.

ANATOMICAL ILLUSTRATIONS

ANATOMICAL ILLUSTRATIONS

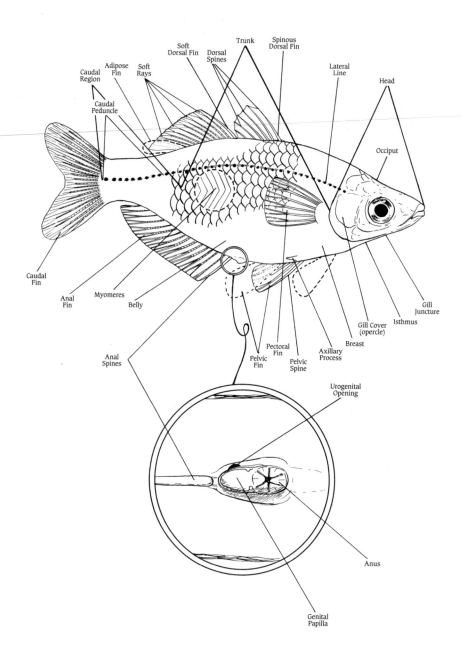

1. External Anatomy of a Fish

ANATOMICAL ILLUSTRATIONS

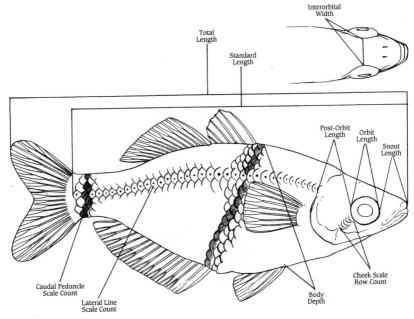

2. Ichthyological Counts and Measurements

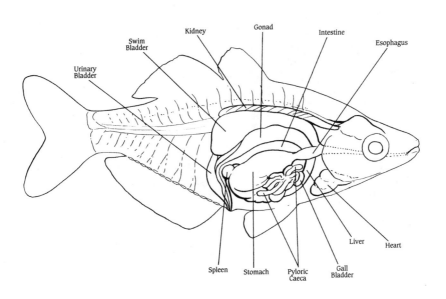

3. Internal Anatomy of a Fish

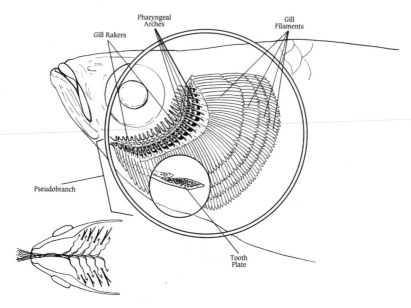

4. Gill Detail

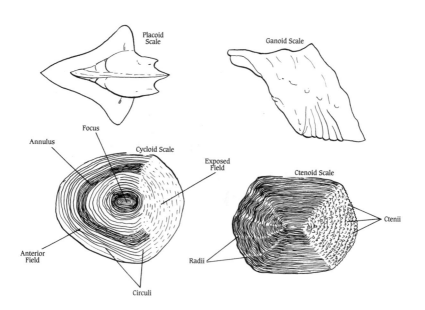

5. Fish Scale Types

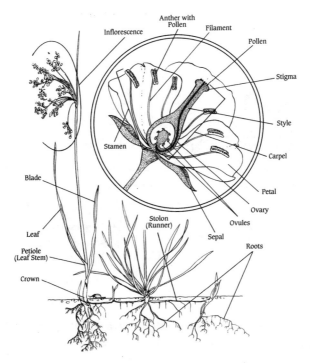

6. *Angiosperm Plant*

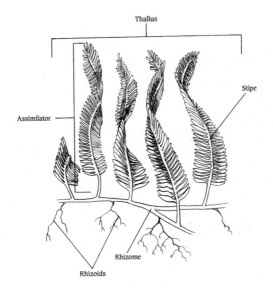

7. *Seaweed*

ANATOMICAL ILLUSTRATIONS

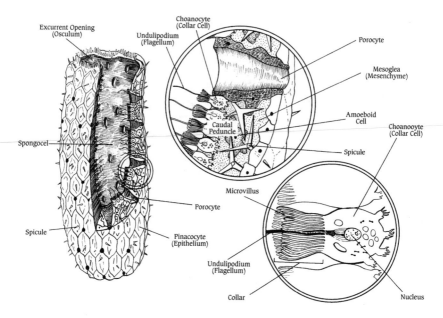

8. Invertebrates: Sponge and Collar Cell Detail

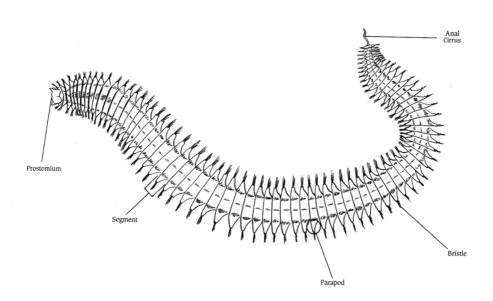

9. Invertebrates: Annelid

ANATOMICAL ILLUSTRATIONS

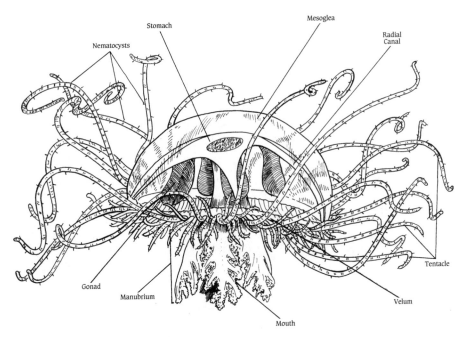

Stomach

Mesoglea

Radial
Canal

Nematocysts

Tentacle

Gonad

Manubrium

Velum

Mouth

10. Invertebrates: Cnidarian, Medusa Form

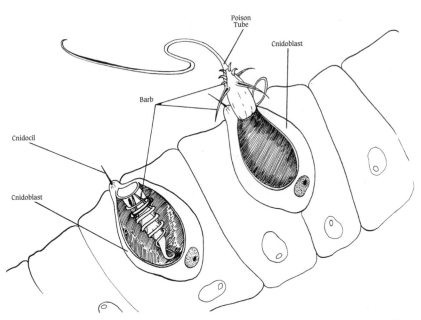

Poison
Tube

Cnidoblast

Barb

Cnidocil

Cnidoblast

11. Invertebrates: Cnidarian, Nematocyst Detail

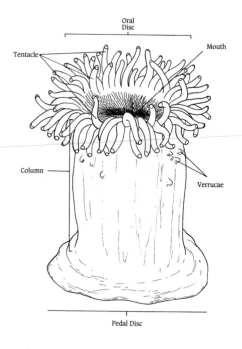

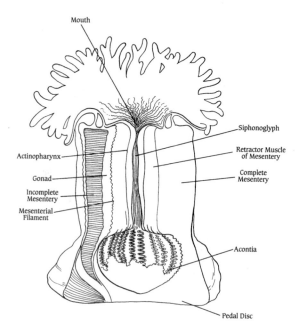

12. *Invertebrates: Cnidarian, Anemone*

ANATOMICAL ILLUSTRATIONS

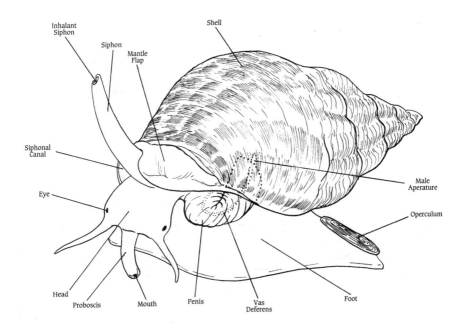

Inhalant Siphon
Siphon
Mantle Flap
Shell
Siphonal Canal
Eye
Male Aperature
Operculum
Head
Proboscis
Mouth
Penis
Vas Deferens
Foot

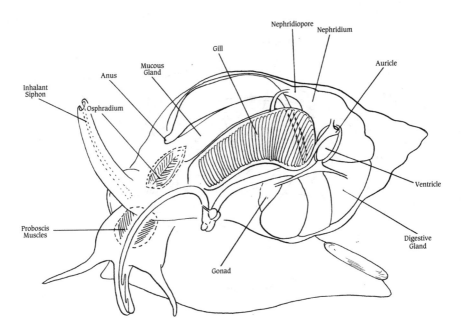

Nephridiopore
Nephridium
Gill
Mucous Gland
Anus
Auricle
Inhalant Siphon
Osphradium
Ventricle
Proboscis Muscles
Digestive Gland
Gonad

13. Invertebrates: Snail

ANATOMICAL ILLUSTRATIONS

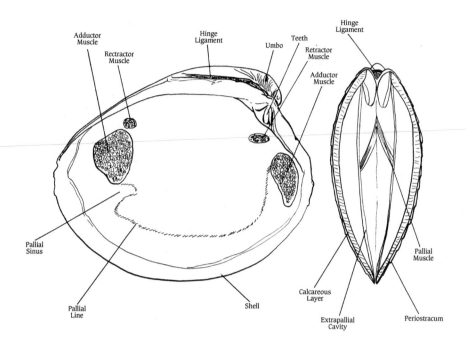

Adductor Muscle
Rectractor Muscle
Hinge Ligament
Umbo
Teeth
Retractor Muscle
Adductor Muscle
Hinge Ligament
Pallial Sinus
Pallial Line
Shell
Calcareous Layer
Extrapallial Cavity
Pallial Muscle
Periostracum

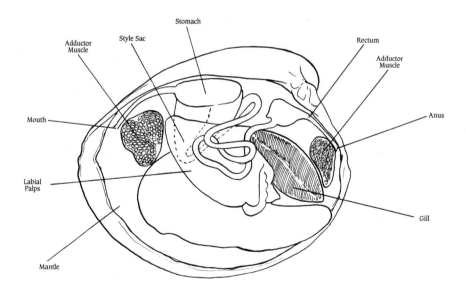

Stomach
Adductor Muscle
Style Sac
Rectum
Adductor Muscle
Mouth
Anus
Labial Palps
Mantle
Gill

14. Invertebrates: Clam

ANATOMICAL ILLUSTRATIONS

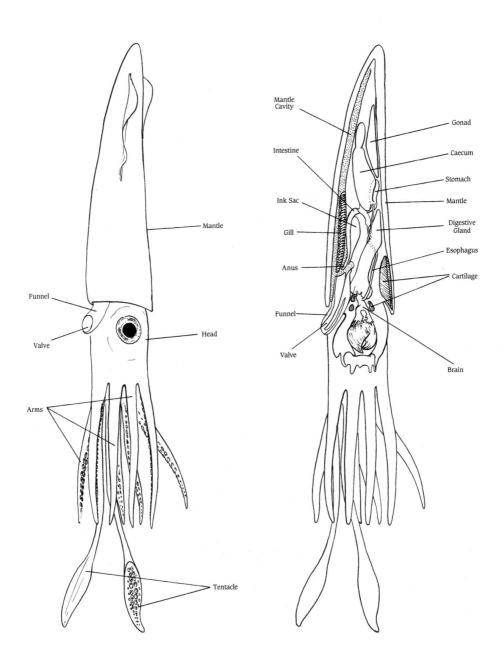

Mantle Cavity

Gonad

Intestine

Caecum

Ink Sac

Stomach

Gill

Mantle

Anus

Digestive Gland

Funnel

Esophagus

Valve

Cartilage

Mantle

Brain

Funnel

Head

Valve

Arms

Tentacle

15. Invertebrates: Squid

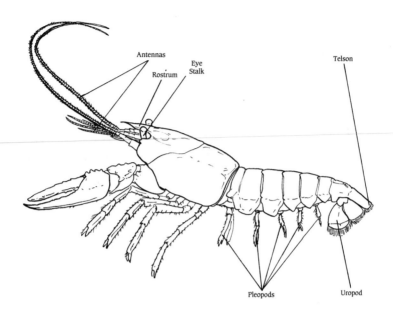

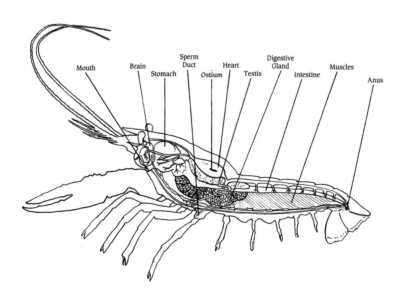

16. Invertebrates: Crustacean

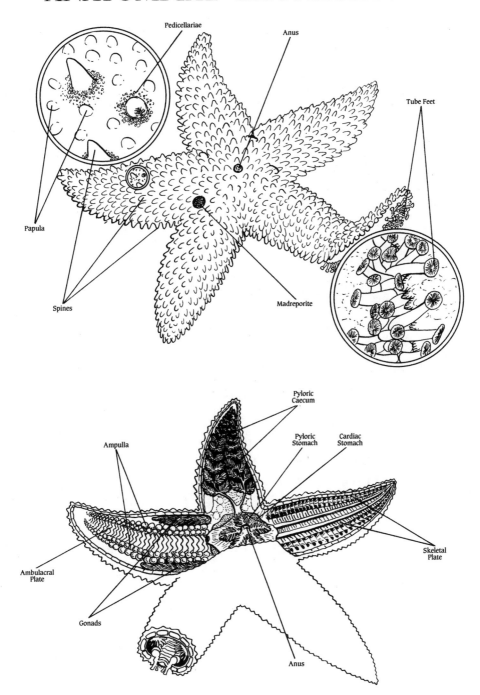

Pedicellariae

Anus

Tube Feet

Papula

Spines

Madreporite

Pyloric Caecum

Ampulla

Pyloric Stomach

Cardiac Stomach

Skeletal Plate

Ambulacral Plate

Gonads

Anus

17. Invertebrates: Sea Star

PRONUNCIATION GUIDE

a = c<u>a</u>t	j = <u>j</u>og
ā = l<u>a</u>ke	k = <u>k</u>id
ä = t<u>ar</u>t	l̩ = <u>l</u>ook
au̇ = c<u>ou</u>nter	m = hi<u>m</u>
b = <u>b</u>ack	n = <u>n</u>ot
ch = <u>ch</u>eck	ŋ = wi<u>ng</u>
d = <u>d</u>og	ō = c<u>o</u>ne
d· = ma<u>tt</u>er	ȯ = c<u>a</u>ll
e = s<u>e</u>t	p = si<u>p</u>
ē = homin<u>y</u>	r = ca<u>r</u>
'ē, ˌē = s<u>ee</u>d	s = me<u>ss</u>
'ə, ˌə = cal<u>e</u>ndar	sh = me<u>sh</u>
ə̇ = antithes<u>i</u>s	t = <u>t</u>ime
ᵊ = catt<u>le</u>	th = <u>th</u>ing
ər = h<u>er</u>b	ü = t<u>oo</u>l
f = <u>f</u>ive	u̇ = m<u>ou</u>nt
g = <u>g</u>ate	v = li<u>v</u>e
h = <u>h</u>ow	w = <u>w</u>alk
hw = <u>wh</u>ite	y = <u>y</u>onder
i = s<u>i</u>p	yü = d<u>ue</u>
ī = k<u>i</u>te	z = <u>z</u>oo

· indicates syllable division within a sequence of sounds that may have more than one syllable division

' precedes syllable with strongest stress

ˌ precedes syllable with next-strongest stress

ⵌ precedes syllable with stress variations between strongest and next strongest

( ) indicates that what is enclosed within or after is present in some vocal expressions but not in others

DICTIONARY OF AQUARIUM TERMS

A

Abramites ('abrəmītəs) — omnivorous South American characins; commonly known as "headstanders" because of the posture they assume while swimming

Acanthophthalmus (ˌaˌkan'thäf'thalməs) — an out-of-date name, often seen in the aquarium literature, for Southeast Asian loaches, Family Cobitidae

Acanthurus (ˌaˌkan'th(y)ùrəs) — type genus of Family Acanthuridae, commonly known as tangs or surgeonfish, herbivorous grazers often found around coral reefs

Acara (¦äkə¦rä) — a name often used in the older aquarium literature for several species of large South American cichlids now assigned to several genera; some species known in the aquarium trade remain undescribed

acclimation — the process of slowly introducing a fish or other organism to new water conditions, usually following transport from one aquarium to the other

acclimation

Acetabularia (ˌasəˌtabyə'la(a)rēə) — a green tropical marine alga commonly known as "mermaid's wineglass" that grows in upright colonies on hard substrates

acid — a chemical compound that dissociates in solution to yield one or more hydrogen ions and a negatively charged ion; a solution with a pH less than 7.0

Acipenser (¦asə¦pen(t)sə(r)) — sturgeons, primitive bony fish found in both freshwater and marine habitats

acontia (ə'känchēə) — filaments extruded from pores at the base of the pedal disc of certain sea anemones, thought to be utilized for defensive purposes

Acorus ('akərəs) — sweet flag, flowering marsh plants of the Family Arum with tough, straplike, emergent leaves that have a pleasant smell when crushed; a cultivar with variegated leaves is often grown in garden ponds

Acropora (ˌakrə'pōrə) — a large genus of branching corals that are typically found in brightly lit waters with high oxygen concentration and heavy turbulence; several species are popular with aquarists owing to the ease with which they can be propagated

acroporid (ˌakrə'pōrəd) — any coral in the Family Acroporidae

acrorhagi (ˌakrə'hagē) — inflated sacs that protrude from beneath the tentacles of certain anemones, bearing stinging cells that prevent other anemones from growing too closely

actinic ((')ak¦tinik) — artificial lighting that is rich in blue wavelengths, used in aquariums to mimic light conditions several meters below the surface

Actinodiscus (ˌaktə(ˌ)nō'diskəs) — corallimorphs or disc anemones, often cultivated by aquarium hobbyists; numerous forms and colors exist

actinopharynx (ˌaktə(ˌ)nō'fariŋ(k)s) — the body opening of cnidarians that serves as both mouth and anus

— actinopharynx

Actinopyga (ˌaktə(ˌ)nō'pīgə) — sea cucumbers found in shallow waters in the tropical Atlantic and Caribbean, popular with aquarists because of their habit of burrowing into the substrate

activated carbon — a filtering medium prepared by exposing organic materials such as bones or coconut shells to high temperatures and steam; this highly porous material absorbs dissolved organic compounds and large ions, such as iodide, from aquarium water

Adamsia ('adəmzē ə) — sea anemones often found living on the mollusk shell occupied by a hermit crab

adductor muscle — in bivalve mollusks, this muscle holds the two halves of the shell together when contracted

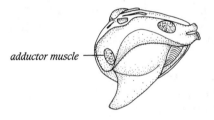
adductor muscle

adenosine triphosphate (ə'denə(ˌ)sēn 'trīfäˌsfāt) — abbreviated as "ATP," a molecule employed by all living cells for transferring energy derived from food metabolism into cellular chemical reactions

(ATP)
adenosine triphosphate

Adinia (ə'dinēə) — an omnivorous killifish found in brackish waters of the southern United States; suitable for a temperate aquarium

adipose fin — a small fin, composed of fatty tissue, located between the dorsal and caudal fins of some fish, notably characins and catfish

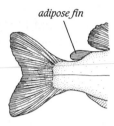

adipose fin

Aequidens ('ēkwə,denz) — flag cichlids, South and Central American species with territorial behavior and undemanding appetite

aged water — 1) tap water that has been left to stand, and from which chlorine has been neutralized; 2) water from a healthy, well-established aquarium that does not contain large amounts of nutrients

ahermatypic (¦ā,hərmə¦tipik) — referring to corals that lack zooxanthellae

Aiptasia ('āp'tā'zēə) — small sea anemones that often multiply to plague proportions in marine aquariums with bright light, heavy loads of organic matter, and excessive nutrients in the water

Aiptasia

air pump — a device for delivering air under low pressure to aquarium equipment connected to it by means of flexible tubing; older models employ a reciprocating piston, while most modern versions use a bellows operated by an electric vibrator to achieve pressurization

airlift — a device that utilizes the principle of displacement for pumping water; forcing air in near the bottom of a tube immersed in the aquarium causes water to be pushed out the top of the tube as the column of air rises

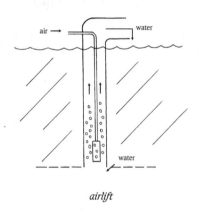

airlift

airstone — any of several types of porous diffusers used to release tiny air bubbles into the aquarium; made of fused sand, fused glass spheres, plastics, or even limewood

air stripping — a synonym for protein skimming

alcyonacean ('alsē'ən,ā,sēən) — a soft coral lacking an axial skeleton

Alcyonium ('alsēə'nēəm) — a typical soft coral without an axial skeleton, popular with aquarists

Alestes ('aləstēs) — omnivorous African characins, such as the nurse tetra, *A. nurse*

algae — any of a wide variety of photosynthetic organisms lacking a vascular system; may be unicellular, filamentous, or, in the case of seaweeds, large and complex in form

algae-eater — any species of fish or invertebrate that feeds on encrusting and filamentous algae; introduced into the aquarium primarily for control of such growths

algal turf scrubber — aquarium water purification system designed at the Smithsonian Institution and employing various species of algae growing on plastic mats in specially designed tanks to remove pollutants from the water

algal turf scrubber

alkalinity — a measure of the ability of a solution to neutralize acid without a change in pH, expressed in milliequivalents per liter (*see* APPENDIX 2: CONVERSION OF OBSERVED HYDROMETER READINGS TO SALINITY)

allelochemicals (ə'lelə,kemə kəls) — substances released into the water by one species that inhibit the growth of one or more potentially competing species, characteristic of some cnidarians kept in minireef aquariums

allopatric (ə'läpa·trik) — literally "different country," referring to the occurence of sister species that are geographically separated although sharing a common ancestor

alpheid ('alfēəd) — a member of the snapping shrimp family, marine crustaceans with one appendage modified for the production of a sudden popping sound that is thought to deter predators; some members have the sound appendage modified for digging, have lost the ability to pop, and rely on partnership with certain fish for protection

Alpheus ('alfēəs) — snapping shrimps, including *A. armatus*, found in association with the anemone *Bartholomea annulata* in the tropical Atlantic

Alternanthera (,ȯltə(r)'nanthərə) — a freshwater flowering plant of the amaranth family of South America used in aquariums for its upright habit and rapid growth

Alveopora (al'vēə,pōrə) — stony corals, Family Poritidae, generally considered difficult to maintain in the aquarium

Amblycirrhites (,amblē'sə'rē'tēs) — hawkfish, Family Cirrhitidae, found in both the Atlantic and Pacific regions

Amblygobius (ˌamblē'gōbēəs) — Indo-Pacific gobies, Family Gobiidae, that typically shelter in the burrow abandoned by another animal, although the most popular aquarium species, *A. rainfordi*, is found near coral heads

amines — chemical compounds containing the amino radical (—NH₂+); amino acids are the chemical units from which proteins are constructed

Ammannia ('amə,nē(y)a) — a fast-growing flowering aquatic plant of the loosestrife family from tropical Africa

ammonium — the ionized form of ammonia (NH₄+)

amoebocytes (ə'mēbə,sīts) — specialized cells in the body of a sponge that are involved in food transport within the animal

amphipod ('amfə,päd) — small, laterally compressed freshwater or marine crustaceans that often are transported into aquariums unintentionally; they are harmless scavengers and are eaten by many types of fish

Amphiprion ('amfip'rēən) — one of two genera of pomacentrid fish that associate with sea anemones; also called clownfish, they are popular with marine aquarium hobbyists

Amplexidiscus (¦am,pleksə¦diskəs) — a single species of corallimorph, commonly referred to as the "giant mushroom polyp," capable of feeding upon small fish that become trapped in its stubby tentacles

ampulla (am'pu̇lə) — part of the water vascular system of echinoderms; like the bulb of a medicine dropper, it forces water into, or draws water from, an individual tube foot

Amyloodinium (ˌamə,lü'dē'nēəm) — a parasitic dinoflagellate that infests the gills and epidermis of many species of marine fish, often fatally; synonyms are "marine velvet" and "coral fish disease"

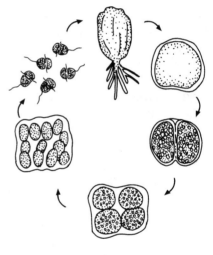

Amyloodinium

anabantid (ˌanə'bantəd) — referring to any of the labyrinth fish, Family Anabantidae, freshwater species characterized by an organ that permits them to breathe atmospheric oxygen

Anableps ('anə,bleps) — type genus of the "four-eyed fish" family; the unique structure of the eyes of these freshwater fish permits them to see above and below the surface simultaneously

anaerobes ('anə,rōbs) —bacteria that do not require oxygen to carry out metabolism; "facultative anaerobes" can survive in the presence of oxygen, while free oxygen is poisonous to "obligate anaerobes"

anal fin — the unpaired fin arising on the midline of the ventral surface of a fish, anterior to the tail and usually just posterior to the anus and urogenital openings

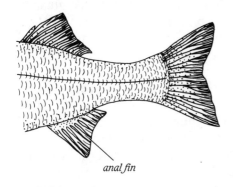

anal fin

Anampses (,anə'm'psəs) — small tropical wrasses, Family Labridae, that feed on benthic invertebrates and are generally difficult to maintain in aquariums

Ancistrus (an'sistrəs) — one of several genera of South American suckermouth catfish, often called "bristle-nosed plecostomus"

anemone (ə'nemənē) — a non-colonial anthozoan with tentacles in multiples of six, lacking a calcified skeletal structure and usually attached to a solid substrate by means of the pedal disc

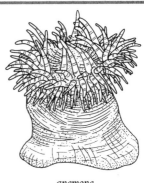

anemone

anemonefish — any of the pomacentrid fish of the genera *Amphiprion* or *Premnas* that associate with sea anemones

angelfish — in fresh water, *Pterophyllum*, South American cichlids that have long been popular with hobbyists; one species, *P. scalare*, exists in many cultivated varieties; a marine angelfish is any member of Family Pomacanthidae, all colorful, including small species of *Centropyge* that generally adapt well to aquarium care, and larger species of *Pomacanthus* and others that can be challenging to maintain in the aquarium

anglerfish — predatory fish in the Family Antennaridae that entice prey within striking distance by means of a "fishing pole" formed from the first dorsal fin spine

angiosperm ('anjēō,spərm) — any flowering plant, referring to the enclosure of the seed within a fruit

Aniculus ('anə,kuləs) — demon hermit crabs, such as the Indo-Pacific *A. strigatus*, adapted to utilize empty mollusk shells whose narrow openings render them unusable by other hermit crabs

anions ('a͵nīəns) — ions bearing a negative electrical charge, such as chloride (Cl⁻)

annelid ('anᵊləd) — any member of the animal phylum Annelida, the segmented worms

Anomalops (ə'nō'mələps) — flashlight fish, an Indo-Pacific species that occurs in two forms depending upon water depth; bioluminescent due to bacteria living within a light organ underneath each eye

Anostomus (ə'nōstə'məs) — omnivorous South American characins; some are known as "headstanders"

anoxic — lacking free oxygen

antenna — the elongated sensory appendage of a crustacean

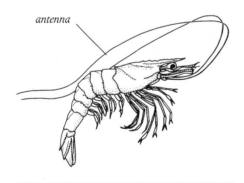
antenna

Antennarius (͵an·͵te'na(a)rēəs) — type genus of anglerfish, Family Antennaridae, marine species that lure prey within striking distance by means of a "fishing pole" formed from the first dorsal fin spine

anterior — referring to the head end of the body of a bilaterally symmetrical animal

Anthelia ((')ant¦hēlyə) — colonial soft corals with feathery tentacles; popular with marine aquarists

Anthias ('an(t)thēəs) — small, colorful sea basses, Family Serranidae, that form large schools and feed on plankton in open waters, suitable for large aquarium displays

Anthopleura (an(t)thə͵plürə) — sea anemones, often tinted green by the presence of symbiotic algae; found off the Pacific coast of North America and elsewhere in the Pacific

anthozoan (͵an(͵)thō'zōən) — literally "flower animal"; any member of Phylum Cnidaria, Class Anthozoa, characterized by the predominance of the flowerlike polyp form in the life cycle

antibiotic — a medication that kills or otherwise halts the reproduction of bacteria

antifoulant — a chemical agent added to paint to prevent encrustation by aquatic organisms such as algae or barnacles

antihelminthic (͵antə'hel¦min(t)thik) — any medication used in the treatment of parasitic infestations by worms

anti-inflammatory — a medication that reduces inflammation, the process by which injured or infected tissues become reddened due to localized expansion of the blood capillaries

antioxidant — a chemical agent that prevents foodstuffs or other perishables from being degraded through exposure to atmospheric oxygen

antiviral — a medication that interferes with replication of a virus, a submicroscopic pathogen that must parasitize a living cell for its own reproduction

Anubias ('ä,nü,bēəs) — semiaquatic plants in the aroid family, native to Africa; sometimes planted in freshwater aquariums

anus — the opening at the posterior end of the gastrointestinal tract through which feces are eliminated

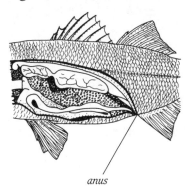

anus

Aphanius (,afə'nēəs) — egg-laying toothed carps of Europe and Asia; kept by specialist aquarium hobbyists

Aphyosemion ((')ā¦fē'ō,semēən) — killifish, or egg-laying toothed carps, Family Cyprinodontidae, of Africa, popular with freshwater aquarium enthusiasts

Apistogramma (ə,pistə'gramə) — dwarf cichlids native to Central and South America that are popular with some aquarium hobbyists because of their small size and relatively nonaggressive nature

Aplocheilus (,aplō'kīləs) — sometimes known as "panchax"; egg-laying toothed carps found on the Indian subcontinent

Aplysia (ə'plizh(ē)ə) — opisthobranch mollusks commonly called "sea hares"

aplysiid (,aplə'sīəd) — any member of the mollusk Family Aplysiidae, or "sea hares," characterized by a reduced internal shell; all are vegetarian grazers

Apogon (ə'pō,gän) — cardinalfish, Family Apogonidae; schooling tropical marine fish, largely nocturnal; popular aquarium species found near coral reefs

Apolemichthys (ə'pälə'mik(t)thəs) — reef-dwelling marine angelfish that feed on sessile invertebrates, making them difficult as aquarium subjects

Aponogeton (,apə(,)nō'jē,tän) — freshwater plants, occuring largely in Asia, that grow from an underground tuber; unlike most other aquarium plants they require a period of dormancy with cool temperatures in order to grow properly

aquaculture — production of aquatic organisms for food, aquarium, or scientific purposes, generally as a commercial venture

aquaculturist — one who practices aquaculture

aquarist — one who designs or maintains an aquarium

aquarium — 1) a tank, often fitted with life-support equipment, specifically constructed for housing living aquatic organisms for exhibition, aquaculture, or scientific study, of dimensions appropriate to enclosure within a building; 2) an exhibit of living organisms in one or several separate containers, intended to give the impression of a window into an aquatic habitat

aquascape — the physical design of the interior of an aquarium, including rocks or other objects selected and placed in such a way as to convey to the viewer the aquarist's impression of an underwater scene

aquatic — of or living in water

Arachnanthus (ˌaˌrakˈnan(t)thəs) — one of several genera of tube-dwelling cnidarians that resemble anemones

aragonite (əˈragəˌnīt) — a form of calcium carbonate deposited as skeletal elements in marine invertebrates such as corals

arborescent — "treelike," usually in reference to the body structure of certain colonial marine invertebrates such as gorgonian soft corals that branch and rebranch

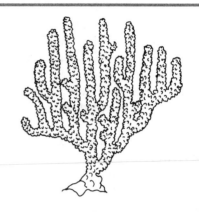

arborescent

arm — among aquarium organisms this term is properly applied only to the appendages of brittlestars or to the body divisions of sea stars

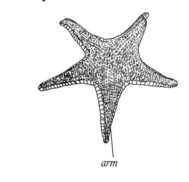

arm

Artemia (ärˈtēmēə) — the genus to which brine shrimp, a popular food for both marine and freshwater aquariums, are assigned

Artemia

arthropod — any member of *Phylum Arthropoda*, invertebrates characterized by jointed appendages and an external skeleton composed of chiton, including the terrestrial insects as well as a variety of marine and freshwater organisms

asexual reproduction — production of offspring without the union of gametes; examples include budding in some cnidarians, regeneration of separated cells of sponges, and rooting cuttings of many types of flowering aquatic plants

Aspidontus (¦aspə͵dōntəs) — Indo-Pacific blennies noted for their mimicry of cleaner wrasses, allowing them to get close enough to other fish to bite them

assimilate — in biology, the incorporation of nutrient molecules into the body structure of the consumer

Astraea (a'strēə) — tropical marine gastropods often collected from Florida for algae control in the aquarium

Astrangia (ə'strānjēə) — star corals, stony corals usually forming small colonies and encrusting rocks; so named for the appearance of the skeletal cups from which the polyps protrude

Astronotus (ə'strə͵nōtəs) — the oscar, *A. ocellatus*, arguably the most popular member of the cichlid family, growing to almost a foot (30 cm) in length and becoming quite tame

Astropecten (͵astrō'pektən) — an Indo-Pacific sea star with large, distinctive spines at the edges of the arms; it feeds at night on small bivalve mollusks

Astrophyton (a'sträfə͵tän) — the Caribbean basket star, a large echinoderm with multibranched arms that are used for capturing plankton; often imported but does poorly in the aquarium

Astyanax (ə'stīə͵naks) — characins of Mexico, Central, and South America, notably the blind cave tetra, *A. fasciatas mexicanus*

Aulonocara ('aùlo'nō͵karə) — peacock cichlids endemic to Lake Malawi, Africa

Aurelia (ȯ'rēlyə) — the common moon jelly, a sea jelly found worldwide and often exhibited in public aquariums

Avrainvillea (ə'vrēn'vilēə) — green tropical seaweeds that grow upright from a base imbedded in the substrate; they have a characteristic texture resembling felt

axial skeleton — the stiffened, proteinaceous internal structure that provides rigidity to the bodies of gorgonians

Azolla (ə'zälə) — mosquito ferns, tiny floating plants commonly grown in both freshwater aquariums and garden ponds

Bacopa (bə'kōpə) — freshwater flowering plants of the snapdragon family with rounded, succulent leaves; usually grown from cuttings

Badis ('bādəs) — a beautiful fish from India that has a single species as its only representative; it feeds on small, meaty foods in standing water with heavy vegetation

baitfish — any of several small species sold for use by anglers or trappers

Balistapus (bə'li(ˌ)stapəs) — triggerfish, Family Balistidae, including the large, aggressive undulated trigger, *B. undulatus*

Balistes (bə'li(ˌ)stēz) — triggerfish, Family Balistidae, including the Atlantic queen trigger, *B. vetula*

Balistoides (bə'li(i)stō(y)dəs) — triggerfish, Family Balistidae, including the clown trigger, *B. conspicillum*

ballast — the transformer that boosts house current to the voltage required for the operation of fluorescent or metal halide aquarium lighting systems

barb — any of numerous small freshwater carps that are popular with hobbyists, naturally ranging from Africa to Southeast Asia

barbels — thin, fleshy appendages near the mouths of certain fish, notably members of the carp and catfish families, that have a sensory function

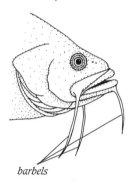

barbels

Barbodes (bärbōds) — a generic name for certain Asian cyprinids; used in older literature but now considered invalid

Barbus ('bärbəs) — cyprinid fish, or barbs, from Southeast Asia, including several frequently kept in aquariums, such as the clown barb, *B. everetti*

Barclaya (bärklā(y)ə) — orchid lily, a member of the water lily family from Southeast Asia that produces a rosette of lance-shaped leaves with ruffled edges; a red form is available for aquarium horticulture

Bartholomea (bärthələmēə) — the sea anemone commonly known as the Curlicue Anemone, owing to the spiral arrangement of stinging cells around its tentacles

base — a chemical compound that acts as the acceptor of electrons from an acid in a neutralization reaction; a solution with a pH greater than 7.0

basslet — any of several marine fish, generally less than four inches in length, in the sea bass family, Serranidae

batfish — any member of the genus *Platax*, marine fish so named because of their elongate, winglike dorsal, pectoral, and anal fins and dark coloration

Batophora (bə'to͵fōrə) — a green marine alga that resembles small bananas attached to a solid surface

Battelaria ('bad·ᵊl(y)ərēə) — small herbivorous snails found in abundance on rocks near the tideline and sometimes imported for algae control in marine aquariums

belly — the ventral portion of the body of a fish, between the pectoral and anal fins

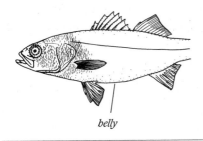

belly

Belontia ('bē͵lon(ch)ēə) — combtails, Family Belontiidae, from Indonesia and India; suitable for a planted aquarium and easily maintained

benthic ('ben(t)thik) — bottom-dwelling organisms, or those that characteristically live upon a solid substrate, such as rocks or corals

Betta — the popular Siamese fighting fish *B. splendens*; related species are seldom seen in the aquarium trade

betta — a synonym for "Siamese fighting fish," derived from the scientific name

bilateral symmetry — trait exhibited by organisms in which there is only one body axis separating similar left and right sides, as in all vertebrate and many invertebrate groups

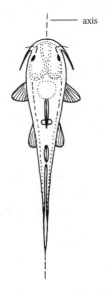

axis

bilateral symmetry

bioaccumulation — the concentration of a chemical substance, such as mercury, at successively higher levels in a food web, or in an individual species

bioball — a spherical plastic object, available in various designs, intended for colonization by nitrifying bacteria in a biological filtration system

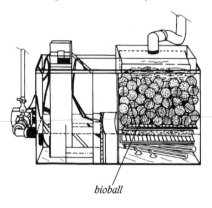

bioball

biodiversity — the total of all living species found with an ecosystem

biogenic — referring to any substance created as a result of the activities of living organisms, for example, petroleum or atmospheric oxygen

biolimiting — said of any factor that prevents the growth of an organism if in short supply

bioload — in an aquarium, the demand placed upon the life-support system as a result of the metabolism of all the organisms present within the tank

bioluminescent — said of any living organism that produces light; numerous invertebrate and microbial groups have this capacity; in fish, bioluminescence may result from symbiotic bacteria or may be produced by specialized tissues

biomass — the total amount by weight of living organisms within a specified area

biotin — a nutrient needed for fatty acid synthesis in plants and animals; essential for photosynthesis

biotope — a specific portion of an ecosystem, defined by the physical conditions and types of organisms usually found, and generally limited in extent, geographically; aquariums are frequently designed to represent a particular biotope

biowheel — a rotating pleated structure over which a stream of water is directed as part of a biological filtration system, and upon which nitrifying bacteria grow

black band disease — a pathological condition observed in stony corals, both in aquariums and in the ocean, thought to be caused by cyanobacteria

blacklight — ultraviolet light, having a wavelength between 100 and 380 nanometers

blackworm — an aquatic annelid about 2 inches (5.1 cm) in length that is sold alive as fish food

Blastomussa (bla'stōmüsə) — stony corals with large polyps and interesting coloration that make them popular with minireef enthusiasts

blastula — a hollow ball of cells formed by the repeated division of a zygote

bleaching — a condition in which the zooxanthellae are lost, rendering the host cnidarian white in color

Blennius ('blenē'ós) — small marine fish, Family Blennidae; often imported for minireef aquariums

blenny — common name for any member of the Family Blennidae

bloodworm — the aquatic larva of a type of gnat; it is bright red in color and is sold frozen as a freshwater fish food

body depth — the maximum distance measured perpendicular to the head-to-tail axis of a fish

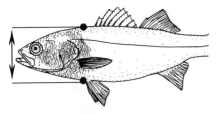

body depth

bog — a constantly moist terrestrial habitat characterized by the presence of sphagnum mosses and acid peat, in which certain wetland plants naturally grow

Bolbitis (bōl'bētəs) — aquatic ferns native to Africa

Bolbometapon (bōl'bō'mətəpon) — parrotfish, Family Scaridae, marine species that bite off chunks of living coral

boron — a chemical element required in trace amounts by many types of living organisms

Botia ('bō(sh)ēə) — genus from Southeast Asia containing several species of loaches ideal for freshwater aquariums

box filter — a simple device for aquarium water purification, usually placed inside the tank, using an airlift to draw water though polyester fiber or other media enclosed within it

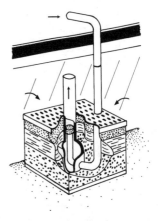

box filter

boxfish — any member of the Ostraciidae, a family of marine fish in which the body is enclosed in a series of interlocking bony plates that provide protection

Brachionus ('brak‚ēə'nəs) — the marine rotifer most often cultured for feeding newly hatched fish larvae

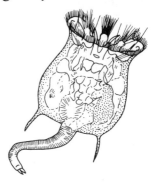

Brachionus

brachiopod ('brakēa,päd) — bivalved invertebrates with unequal shells that are found attached to rocks in marine habitats

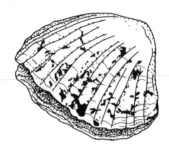

brachiopod

Brachydanio ('brakē(y)ə'dānē,ō) — the zebra danio; a carplike fish popular with freshwater hobbyists for decades, and its close relatives

brackish — describing water that is less salty than seawater, but not yet fresh, as occurs naturally in estuaries

branchlet — the outermost extension of the body of any organism with a treelike growth form

breast — in fish, the portion of the ventral body surface lying between the isthmus and the insertion point of the pelvic fins

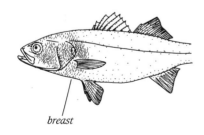

breast

breeding — successful spawning and rearing of offspring of any variety

of aquarium fish; frequently the goal of an advanced hobbyist

Briereum ('brīə(r)ēəm) — soft corals that lack skeletal elements and that encrust solid substrates; popular with minireef enthusiasts due to their rapid growth rate

brine shrimp — *Artemia salina* and its close relatives, crustaceans often used as food for both freshwater and marine aquarium inhabitants

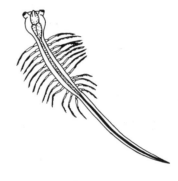

brine shrimp

bristle — short, thick, hairlike epidermal outgrowths, often pointed on the distal end, and sometimes hollow and venomous; found on certain marine annelids

bristle

bristleworm — marine annelids with setae, or bristles, along the length of the body; generally considered an aquarium pest because some species feed on corals

bristleworm

brittlestar — any member of the echinoderm class Ophiuroidea, in which there are multiple arms, usually five, extending radially from a central, disk-shaped body; the name derives from the ease with which some species are damaged by handling

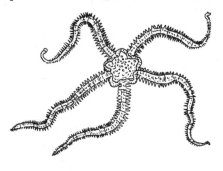

brittlestar

bromide — ionic form of the element bromine (Br⁻), required in small amounts by many types of organisms

brood — a group of sibling offspring arising from a clutch of eggs of any species of fish or invertebrate

brood pouch — a specialized invagination of the abdomen of the male seahorse, in which fertilized eggs develop and are nourished by a placentalike structure

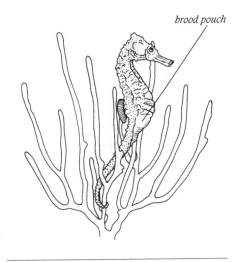

brood pouch

Brooklynella ('brŭklə¸nələ) — a protozoan parasite infesting the epidermis of marine fish, especially those in the genus *Amphiprion*, commonly known as "clownfish disease"; the condition is abetted by crowding and poor water conditions, but often responds to treatment with medications containing malachite green

bryozoan (¦brīə¦zō¸en) — any member of the Phylum Bryozoa, filter-feeding marine invertebrates with an encrusting growth form typically found on live rock; the few freshwater species are of no interest to aquarium hobbyists

bubble nest — a floating raft of air bubbles and sometimes aquatic plants, held together by an oral secretion, in which the eggs of some fish are placed for incubation and are guarded by the male parent

bubble nest

budding — a form of reproduction in certain corals and anemones, in which fully formed offspring are formed as an outgrowth of the body of the parent organism

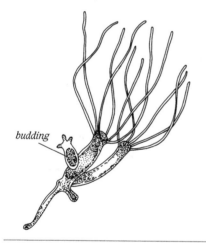

budding

buffer — a solution of chemical compounds and water that resists a change in pH when either acid or alkali is added

Bunocephalus (ˌbyünəˈsēfaləs) — South American catfish whose body shape has given rise to the common name "banjo catfish"

butterflyfish — any fish of the marine Family Chaetodontidae, found exclusively in association with coral reefs; many are delicate and difficult to feed, but a few species make excellent aquarium subjects; a single freshwater species, *Pantodon bucholzi*, though unrelated, is commonly known as the "African butterflyfish"

Cabomba (ke'bämbə) — vinelike aquatic plants with feathery, dark green foliage and tiny white flowers borne at the surface; they require very bright light to thrive under aquarium conditions

calcareous (kal'ka(a)rēəs) — having calcium carbonate incorporated into a body structure, such as skeletal elements or a shell

calcification — 1) the process by which calcium carbonate is incorporated into the body structure of a living organism; 2) the deposition of calcium carbonate as a mineral through chemical processes taking place in aquatic habitats

Calcinus (ˌkalsə'nůs) — hermit crabs popular with hobbyists because of their small size and bright coloration; usually added to the marine aquarium for algae control

calcium carbonate — CaCO₃, a crystalline solid, insoluble in water, incorporated into supportive or protective structures in many animal and plant species

calcium reactor — a device for increasing the content of calcium ions in the water of a marine aquarium that functions by passing acidified water over pieces of calcium carbonate-containing materials, such as shell fragments

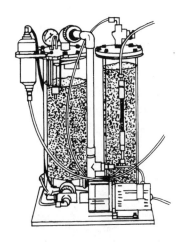

calcium reactor

calcium supplement — any chemical added to a marine aquarium to increase the calcium content of the water

Calliactis (ˌkalēək'təs) — an anemone occurring along the Atlantic and Gulf coasts of the United States; often found attached to the shell inhabited by a hermit crab

Calloplesiops (ˌkalə'pləsēops) — comet groupers, sea basses with nocturnal habits and flowing fins that have been propagated successfully in the aquarium

calyx ('kāliks) — 1) botanically, the portion of a flower that supports the petals and is comprised of the sepals; 2) zoologically, the cuplike structure of a colonial coral from which the individual polyp protrudes and into which it can usually be withdrawn

canines — fangs found in many vertebrates, including some fish, and used for piercing and holding prey; generally, these teeth are best developed in carnivorous species

canister filter — an aquarium filter in which the media are enclosed in a plastic can located external to the tank, with water entering and leaving the can through hoses leading to and from the aquarium

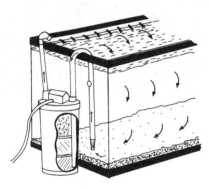

canister filter

Capoeta (ˌkapōdə) — cyprinids of Europe and western Asia, of limited interest to specialized aquarium hobbyists; the name is sometimes incorrectly applied to other cyprinids in the aquarium trade

carapace ('karəˌpās) — the exoskeleton covering all or part of the dorsal surface of a crustacean, or the shell of a turtle

Carapus ('karəpəs) — the pearlfish, rarely imported for the aquarium, that lives in the gut of a sea cucumber, emerging at night to feed on small invertebrates

Carassius (ka'rasēəs) — the common goldfish and all its many aquarium and pond varieties

carbon dioxide — a colorless, odorless gas (CO_2), formed along with water during food metabolism by the majority of living organisms; accumulation in aquarium water is to be avoided because of toxic effects on fish; it is absorbed by plants during photosynthesis and eliminated by aeration and buffering

carbonic acid — the compound that results when carbon dioxide dissolves in water

carboy — a large bottle, useful for the storage and dispensing of chemicals or for culturing certain types of aquarium foods

Cardamine (kär'damə(ˌ)nē) — a freshwater angiosperm known as Chinese ivy, usually grown from rooted stem cuttings

cardinalfish — any of the marine species in the Family Apogonidae

Carnegiella ('kärnəgē'lə) — hatchetfish, surface-dwelling South American characins that can actually "fly" short distances in pursuit of insect prey

carnivore — an organism that feeds principally upon animals

carotenoid (kə'rät°n,óid) — one of several yellow colored organic molecules important in pigment development and cellular metabolism, such as vitamin A

cartilage — a tough, flexible tissue containing the protein collagen that forms all of the skeletal system of elasmobranch fish and a portion of the skeletal structure of all other vertebrate animals

Cassiopeia (¦kasēə¦ō'pē(y)ə) — upside-down sea jellies; schyphozoan cnidarians that orient themselves upside down to expose their symbiotic algae to sunlight

Catalaphyllia (,kad·ə'filēə) — a single species, *C. jardinieri*, called "elegance coral" by minireef enthusiasts; its geographical range is restricted to the Coral Sea near Indonesia

catfish — one of a large number of species in several families sharing the traits of elongated sensory barbels, a scaleless skin sometimes protected by bony plates, and usually a bottom-dwelling habit

cations ('kad·,īəns) — atoms or molecules that bear a positive charge resulting from the loss of one or more electrons

catkin — an inflorescence produced by certain angiosperms, so named

because of the superficial resemblance to a cat's tail

caudal fin — the tail fin of a fish, used primarily for locomotion in the majority of species

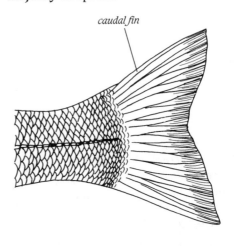

caudal fin

caudal peduncle — the fleshy posterior portion of a fish's body to which the caudal fin is attached

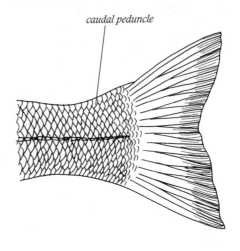

caudal peduncle

caudal peduncle scale count — the number of scales along an imaginary line encircling the most slender portion of this region

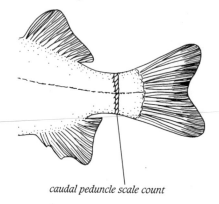

caudal peduncle scale count

Caulastrea ('kȯ'lastrēə) — trumpet coral, a stony coral of easy culture in marine reef aquariums

Caulerpa (kȯ'lərpə) — macroscopic green marine algae often cultivated in hobbyist aquariums, and characteristically possessing an upright, leafy portion arising from a runner that grows over or through a substrate; worldwide in distribution

Centrarchus (sen·'trärkəs) — sunfish of North America, Family Centrarchidae, several species of which adapt easily to aquarium care

Centriscus (sen·'triskəs) — shrimpfish, Family Centriscidae, often found swimming snout downward among the spines of sea urchins, feeding upon plankton; exhibited in specialized aquariums as a curiosity

Centropyge (sen·(ˌ)trō'pīgə) — dwarf marine angelfish with approximately 15 species imported for the aquarium trade; moderately easy to keep, requiring a diet rich in vegetable

matter; these fish often spawn in hobbyist tanks but to date have not been successfully reared to maturity

cephalopod ('sefələˌpäd) — a member of the molluscan class Cephalopoda, including octopus, squid, argonauts, and the chambered nautilus

cephalothorax (ˌsefə'läˌthȯrˌaks) — the anterior portion of the body of a crustacean to which the feeding appendages and antennae are attached

cephalothorax

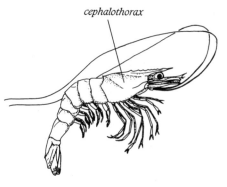

cerata (ˌserə'tə) — outgrowths of the body of certain species of nudibranchs, or sea slugs, that function variously in camouflage, defense, or nutrition; some slugs merely resemble their prey organism in appearance, while others commandeer stinging or photosynthetic cells, transferring them to these structures for the slug's subsequent use

cerata

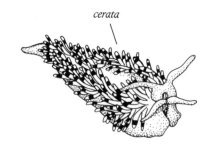

Ceratophyllum (ˌserə(ˌ)tōˈfīləm) — hornworts, common and hardy floating plants for freshwater aquariums and ponds

Ceratopteris (ˌserəˈtäptərə̇s) — floating or rooted freshwater ferns that are popular aquarium plants, able to produce plantlets from the margins of larger leaves

cerebellum — the portion of the vertebrate brain, located posterior to the cerebrum, controlling muscular coordination

cerebrum — the portion of the vertebrate brain responsible for sensory perception and voluntary movement, as well as higher cognitive functions

Cerianthus (ˌsirēˈan(t)ˈthəs) — a tube-dwelling cnidarian superficially resembling a sea anemone; sometimes imported for the aquarium; predatory on fishes

Cespitularia (sesˈpitülərēə) — stoloniferan soft corals with branched colonies

Cetoscarus (ˌsēd·əˈskərəs) — one of several genera of parrotfish, Family Scaridae, imported for aquarium exhibition

Chaca (chəˈkä) — flattened, nocturnal, predatory catfish of India and Southeast Asia, with undemanding aquarium needs

Chaetodon (kēˈtēˌdän) — type genus of the butterflyfish family, Chaetodontidae, a marine group found only in association with coral reefs; a few species make good aquarium specimens, although the majority do not adapt well to captive conditions

Chalceus (ˈkalsəs) — predatory South American characins with silvery scales and often a bright pink tail fin

Chanda ((ˌ)chənˈdä) — glassfish; small perciform Asian species noted for its transparency

Channa (ˈkanə) — snakeheads, predatory freshwater fish from southern China and India exhibited alone in large aquariums

characin (ˈkəˈrəsə̇n) — any fish in the Family Characidae, some commonly called tetras; found in South America and Africa, they vary greatly in size, appearance, and ecology

cheek row scale count — the number of scales along an imaginary line connecting the eye to the anterior edge of the gill cover

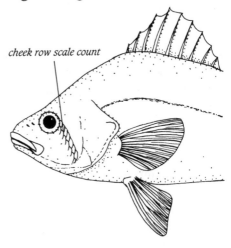

cheek row scale count

Cheirodon ('kīrō'dȯn) — small South American characin; the cardinal tetra, a popular fish for the community freshwater tank, originally assigned to this genus, now is known as *Paracheirodon axelrodi*

chelae ('kēl(ˌ)lē) — singular: chela; the often enlarged anterior appendages, or "pincers," of crustaceans and arachnids

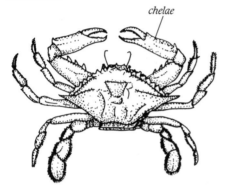

chelae

Chelmon (kel'mȯn) — a popular marine species with an orange-and-white-banded pattern; the copperband butterflyfish, *C. rostratus*, feeds with its elongated snout on small invertebrates

chemical attractants — compounds released into the water that stimulate another organism or cell to move toward the releasing organism or cell; females may release an attractant for sperm cells of the same species, for example

chemical defenses — compounds that effect protection upon their possessor, including poison, secreted within the body, venom, a poison introduced into another organism, or substances that mask the organism's presence from a predator

chemical filtration — the removal of dissolved compounds from aquarium water by foam fractionation or adsorption on various media

chemoreceptors ('kemō·rȯ'septǝ(r)s) — specialized cells or subcellular components recognizing specific types of chemical signals, as in the olfactory epithelium of fish, or on the antennae of crustaceans

Chilodonella (ˌkīlǝdǝ'nelǝ) — a ciliated protozoan parasite of freshwater fish, usually of coldwater species such as goldfish, that destroys epithelial tissue and is often fatal if untreated

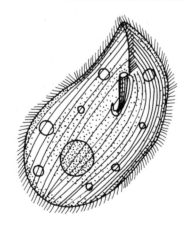

Chilodonella

chitin ('kītˀn) — a tough, proteinaceous material found abundantly in the external skeleton of arthropods; also occurs in such diverse organisms as fungi and mollusks

chiton ('kītˀn) — any of numerous species of primitive mollusks characterized by a shell consisting of a series of eight calcified plates, Class Amphineura; most species attach themselves to a solid substrate and move about at night to graze on algae

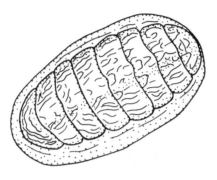

chiton

Chlamys ('klaməs) — bivalved mollusks with circular, rough-surfaced shells sometimes attached to live rock specimens collected for marine reef aquariums

chloramine (ˌklōrˌamīn) — a chemical often used in the treatment of municipal water supplies that must be removed from aquarium water by activated carbon treatment or by addition of an appropriate counteracting chemical

Chlorella (klə'relə) — a unicellular green marine alga often cultured as a food for invertebrates or fish larvae

chlorine remover — usually sodium thiosulfate, or any chemical agent employed to eliminate toxic chlorine from municipal tap water before using it in an aquarium

chlorophyll — one of a group of green pigments that permit photosyn-

thetic organisms to utilize the energy of sunlight for food production

chloroplast — a subcellular structure found in photosynthetic organisms containing chlorophyll and in which photosynthesis takes place

chlorotic (klə'rädik) — a condition seen in vascular plants receiving insufficient iron, in which the leaf veins are bright green while the remainder of the leaf turns yellow

choanocyte ('kōə(ˌ)nō,sīt) — a cell with a characteristic collar surrounding its single flagellum found in sponges; it traps microscopic food from the water passing through the porous body

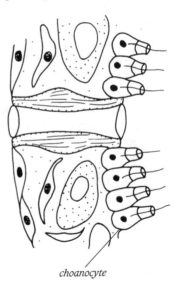

choanocyte

Chondrilla (kän'drilə) — chicken liver sponge, a common, easily cultivated species found on rocks from Florida and the Caribbean

chordate ('kȯrdət) — a member of Phlyum Chordata, characterized by the presence of a stiffening rod of cartilage, the notochord; in vertebrates the notochord is present in the embryo and is replaced by the vertebral column

Chromidotilapia ('krōmə,dó,tə, ləpēə) — territorial West African cichlids that can be maintained in planted aquariums, unlike many members of their family

Chromis ('krōməs) — marine pomacentrid fish typically living in large shoals and feeding on planktonic organisms; several species are regularly imported and can be successfully maintained in aquariums

Chrysiptera (krə'sip(,)tərə) — a pomacentrid genus represented by the popular orange-tailed blue damselfish, *C. cyanea*

Cichlasoma (,siklə'sōmə) — Central American cichlids of moderate size; the genus is currently undergoing taxonomic revision

cichlid ('siklə̇d) — any member of the large freshwater fish Family Cichlidae, distributed from Central and South America to Africa and Asia; a wide variety of feeding and habitat preferences may be found in this group, but the numerous species are united by anatomical similarities and extensive parental care of the eggs and young

cilia ('silēə̇) — numerous short, hairlike projections from the cells of certain protists and the epithelial cells of many types of animals; their rhythmic beating sets up water currents utilized by the organism for movement or food capture, or both

ciliary ('silē,erē) — of or having to do with the cilia, as in "ciliary movement creates water currents"

ciliate ('silēə̇t) — a protist bearing cilia

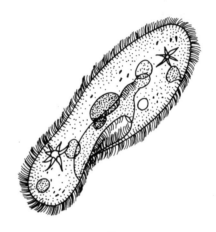

ciliate

circumtropical — referring to the distribution of a species or phenomenon that may be found worldwide between the Tropic of Cancer and the Tropic of Capricorn

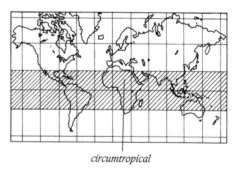

circumtropical

Cirrhilabrus (sə̇'riləbrəs) — social wrasses, Family Labridae, marine fish that are usually found in small shoals consisting of a single, dominant male and several juvenile males and females; numerous, brilliantly colored species are popular with advanced hobbyists

Cirrhipectes (ˌsə̇ˈrēˈpəktēs) — Indo-Pacific blennies, Family Blennidae, characterized by a row of cirri on the nape, often found on surf-swept ridges among algae or branching corals; herbivorous species are suitable for minireef aquariums

cirri (ˌsirˌrī) — singular, cirrus; short, bristlelike projections from the epidermis of certain invertebrates and fish; in blennies, the cirri are often referred to as "eyelashes"

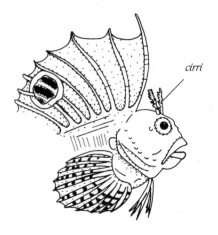
cirri

Cladiella (kləˈdīəlä) — an alcyonarian type of soft coral frequently maintained by minireef enthusiasts

Clarias (kla(a)rēəs) — the walking catfish, *C. batrachus*, once imported as a novelty for freshwater aquariums; it has become a pest species in Florida because of its ability to move overland from one lake or pond to another

Clavularia (ˈklāvəˌlərēə) — encrusting, stoloniferan soft corals readily propagated in a minireef aquarium

cleaner — a marine fish or invertebrate that characteristically removes parasitic organisms and dead tissue from the skin of fish that present themselves at the animal's "cleaning station," often in response to a ritualized "dance" carried out by the cleaner; the phenomenon is sometimes called "cleaning symbiosis," since the cleaner typically feeds on the material it removes from the fish

Clibanarius (klīˈbənˌərēəs) — marine hermit crabs of the tropical Atlantic and Caribbean; the most popular species is the tiny blue-leg hermit, *C. tricolor*, kept in marine tanks for algae control

clonal — referring to the asexual reproduction of a single individual, producing offspring that are genetically identical to the parent

clownfish — originally, referring only to *Amphiprion ocellaris*, but now any of the pomacentrid fish that associate with sea anemones, also known as "anemonefish"

clutch — a mass or cluster of eggs deposited by a fish or invertebrate, often but not always receiving protective care from one or both parents

cnidarian (nīˈdaˌirēən) — any member of Phylum Cnidaria, invertebrates having a three-layered body lacking clearly defined organs, a single opening serving as both mouth and anus, and a ring of tentacles surrounding the opening that bear specialized stinging cells

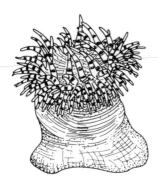

cnidarian

cnidoblast ('nīdə,blast) — the stinging cells of cnidarians, containing the nematocyst

coelenterate (sə̇,lentə'rāt·ə) — a synonym for "cnidarian," now outdated

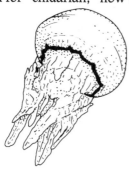

coelenterate

coelom ('sēləm) — the body cavity formed in higher organisms by the division of the embryonic mesodermal tissue layer, and within which the organs are suspended from sheets of tissue called "mesenteries"

cold-blooded — said of organisms whose body temperature is the same as that of their surroundings

Colisa (kə'lēsə) — dwarf gouramis such as *C. lalia*, small labyrinth fish from India with attractive coloration

collar cell — a synonym for choanocyte

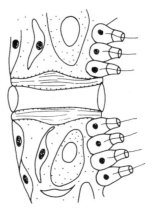

collar cell

Colossoma (kə'läsōmə) — black pacus, vegetarian relatives of the piranhas, Family Characidae, that grow to an enormous size and thus are suitable only for large aquariums

column — the stalk supporting the tentacular crown of a polyp, especially an anemone

column

comb jelly — common name for members of Phylum Ctenophora, invertebrates that resemble cnidarians but lack stinging cells and possess a series of ciliated plates on the body surface

commensalism — a symbiotic relationship in which two species co-occur but neither helps or harms the other

conceptacle — reproductive structure of certain red algae, Phylum Rhodophyta, useful in identification

Condylactis (kən'dīləktəs) — a tropical sea anemone from the Atlantic and Caribbean region, typically found in grass beds or near coral reefs, and regularly imported for the aquarium

congeners — organisms sharing the same genetic background

contractile poylps (kən·'traktəl 'päləps) — individuals within a colony of hydrozoans that are specialized for drawing captured prey toward the mouth

Conus ('kōnəs) — tropical gastropod mollusks capable of delivering a poisonous sting

Convolutriloba (,känvə'lütrīlōbə) — a flatworm pest, recognizable by its distinctive three-pointed posterior; it feeds on aquarium cnidarians

Copella (,kōpə'lə) — South American pyrrhulinid characin, including *C. arnoldi*, that lays its eggs on leaves located above the water surface; the male subsequently moistens them by repeated splashing with his fins

copepod ('kōpə,päd) — tiny crustaceans found in a variety of aquatic habitats and often able to reproduce in the aquarium; free-living forms are eaten by a variety of fish, a few, such as the freshwater "anchor worm," are parasitic

copepod

copper — a chemical element required in trace amounts by many organisms; it is also used in the treatment of protozoan parasite infestations of marine fish and sometimes for control of undesirable algae or mollusks in freshwater aquariums

Coradion (kə,rā dē ən) — the orange-banded coralfish, Family Chaetodontidae, often imported from Indonesia where it occurs in areas of poor coral growth

coral — any of the colonial anthozoans, but most frequently applied to the Order Scleractinia, or stony corals, in which a calcified skeleton is produced

coral reef — an ecosystem associated with a massive underwater structure comprised of the skeletons of stony corals

coral rock — the fossil remains of coral reefs formed prior to the most recent Ice Age

coral sand — granular aggregate of pulverized coral rock, shell fragments, and other minerals deposited on the sea bottom

corallimorpharian (ˌkȯrə'lē,mȯ(r)fərēən) — any member of the anthozoan Order Corallimorpharia, commonly known as false corals or disk anemones

Corallina (ˌkȯrə'līnə) — red marine algae having a calcified skeleton

coralline ('kȯrəˌlīn) — referring to any of the marine algae that possess calcified skeletons

corallite ('kȯrəˌlīt) — an individual polyp of a colonial anthozoan

Coris (kə'rēs) — tropical wrasses, Family Labridae, popular with marine aquarium hobbyists due to the gaudy coloration of the adult males; many species are imported

Cornularia (ˌkȯrnyə'lärēə) — stoloniferan soft corals occasionally imported for minireef aquariums

Corydoras (kə'rəˌdȯrəs) — the most popular armored catfish native to South America; they are frequently included in community freshwater tanks because of their ability to scavenge food from the gravel substrate

courtship — a set of ritual behaviors that permits coordination of spawning behavior between males and females of a species, usually taking place just prior to the deposition of eggs and their fertilization

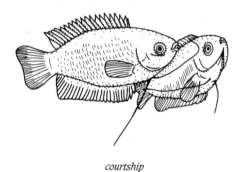

courtship

cowery — any marine gastropod of Family Cypraeidae, recognizable by a colorful, highly polished shell completely enveloped by the mantle

Crenicichla (krȧnəˌsiklə) — the pike cichlids of South America that require a roomy tank because of their aggressive and predatory behavior

crepuscular (krȧ'pəsk(y)ələ(r)) — active primarily at dusk or just before dawn

crinoid ('krīˌnȯ(y)d) — a feather star, or member of the echinoderm Class Crinoidea; sometimes imported; most are too delicate to adapt to aquarium life

Crinum ('krīnəm) — bog lily, a large, bulb-forming plant in the *Amaryllis* family with fragrant white

flowers often grown in ornamental ponds

crushed coral — coral rock that has been milled to granules approximately ¹/₈ inch (3.2 mm) in diameter; used as a substrate material in marine aquariums

crustacean (¦krə¦stāshən) — any member of the arthropod Phylum Crustacea, marine or freshwater animals characterized by jointed appendages, an external skeleton, and a body divided into the externally unsegmented cephalothorax and a segmented abdomen

crustose ('krə₁stōs) — said of algae or colonial invertebrates that form a thin, hard layer on a solid substrate

cryptic coloration — a pattern of pigmentation that allows an organism to blend into the background of its preferred habitat

cryptic coloration

Cryptocaryon (₁kriptə'ka(a)rēən) — a ciliated protozoan infesting the gills and epidermis of marine fish,

commonly known as "white spot" or "marine ich"; it responds to copper treatment

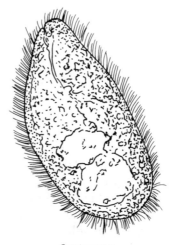

Cryptocaryon

Cryptocentrus (₁kriptə'sen·trəs) — watchman gobies, marine fish often found in association with certain species of alpheid shrimps

Cryptocoryne (₁kriptə'kȯrīn) — a large genus of tropical freshwater flowering plants of the aroid family, imported from Asia and popular with aquarists

Cryptodendrum (kriptə'dəndrəm) — an unusual and rarely seen anemone that sometimes hosts clownfish

Ctenochaetus (₁te'nō₁kātəs) — bristletooth surgeonfish, Family Acanthuridae, imported primarily from Hawaii and valued for their propensity to consume filamentous algae

ctenoid scale — a scale with small, toothlike projections, giving the fish a rough feel

ctenoid scale

ctenophore ('tenə,fō(ə)r) — any member of Phylum Ctenophora, characterized by a single body opening, no distinct organs, and a series of ciliated plates surrounding the body

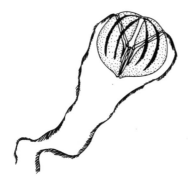

ctenophore

Ctenopoma (,tenə'pōmä) — anabantids of tropical West Africa, suitable for planted aquariums with soft water

current — one-directional movement within a mass of water or air

cyanoacrylate glue ('sīə(,)nō'akrə,lāt glü) — a type of adhesive that adheres well to living tissue; it can be used to attach living coral colonies, for example, to a piece of rock

cyanobacteria ('sīə(,)nō'bak,tirēə) — photosynthetic prokaryotes commonly called "blue green algae," which are often considered pests in both freshwater and marine aquariums

cycling — establishing a population of beneficial nitrifying bacteria in an aquarium's biological filtration system; the name comes from the ecological term "nitrogen cycle"

cycloid scale — a scale with circular bony ridges, found on most types of modern fish

cycloid scale

Cyclops ('sī,kläps) — a genus of copepods with a single eyespot located in the middle of the head

Cyclops

Cymopolia ('sī͵mō͵pəlēə) — calcified tropical marine green alga with a skeletal structure resembling a string of beads and bearing tufts of green, photosynthetic filaments at the ends of the strands

Cynarina ('sinərinə) — a solitary stony coral that lies on sandy or muddy substrates and adapts well to the minireef aquarium

Cynolebias (sinō͵lēbēəs) — a popular genus of annual killifish from South America that live in temporary bodies of water

Cyphoma (͵sīfōmə) — flamingo tongue snails, tropical gastropods that feed on gorgonian soft corals and are sometimes accidentally introduced into the aquarium

Cyprinella (sə'prinələ) — carplike fish of North American streams and rivers, some species of which are exhibited in temperate aquariums

Cyprinodon (sə'prinə͵dän) — cyprinodontids of the United States and Mexico, including the common sheepshead minnow of the eastern coastal marshes, and the rare and endangered pupfish of the desert Southwest

Cyprinus (sə'prīnəs) — the common carp, or koi, *C. carpio*, often maintained in garden ponds

dace ('dās) — any of several species of North American and European cyprinids in various genera, including *Erythrogaster*, *Rhinichthys*, and others

damselfish — pomacentrid fish not associated as adults with anemones, they may be either solitary and territorial, or schooling forms; solitary types are often kept by beginning marine aquarium hobbyists because they are widely available, colorful, and extremely hardy

Danio ('dāneō) — small cyprinids of the Indian subcontinent, including the Giant Danio, *D. aequipinnatus*

danio — any of the cyprinid fish in the genera *Danio* and *Brachydanio*, native to Asia and popular choices for freshwater community aquariums

Daphnia ('dafnēə) — the most commonly encountered genus of water fleas, often cultivated as food for freshwater aquarium fish or their fry

Daphnia

Dardanus ('där¦dānəs) — tropical marine hermit crabs imported from Hawaii and the Indo-Pacific, and maintained primarily for their beautifully colored appendages; *D. megistos*, the Halloween hermit, has bright orange and black stripes

dartfish — any of the gobies in the genera *Nemateleotris* or *Ptereleotris*

Dascyllus ('dasiləs) — humbugs, several widely available damselfish from the Indo-Pacific region

Dasyatis (ˌdasē'adəs) — type genus of the stingray family, Dasyatidae, elasmobranchs with a flattened body and one or more venomous spines on the tail; found worldwide

Dasycladus (ˌdasəˈklədəs) — marine alga commonly found on live rock specimens, resembling an upright bottle brush a few inches tall

Datinoides ('dādˌənˌo(y)dəs) — former name, widely used in the aquarium literature, for *Coius*, the tigerfish, large predators found in brackish waters of the Malaysian peninsula

daylength — the period of time during which there is sufficient sunlight for photosynthesis to take place

decapod ('dekəˌpäd) — crustaceans having five pairs of locomotory appendages

dechlorinator — an agent added to tap water to eliminate harmful chlorine

degrees of hardness — divisions on an arbitrary scale for expressing the amount of dissolved carbonates of calcium and magnesium present in a sample of water (*see also* APPENDIX 1: MEASUREMENTS, EQUIVALENTS, AND FORMULAS)

Dendrochirus (¦den(ˌ)drō͵kərəs) — dwarf lionfish, Family Scorpaenidae; seldom over 6 inches (15 cm) in length, they feed mostly on crustaceans and are venomous

Dendronephthya (¦den(ˌ)drō͵nəf͵th(y)ēə) — spectacularly colored soft corals that are challenging to maintain in the aquarium because they feed primarily upon unicellular marine algae

denitrator — a device for removing nitrate ions from aquarium water

denitrification — the process by which anaerobic bacteria convert nitrate ions into nitrogen gas

denitrifier — any species of bacteria able to convert nitrate ions into nitrogen gas

dentition — the teeth of a particular species, or of a particular portion of the jaw

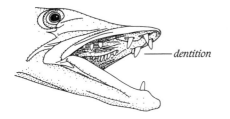
dentition

depigmentation — loss of coloration; bleaching

desalination — removal of dissolved solids from seawater, usually to produce potable water

dessication — dehydration; drying out

detritus (də·trīd·əs) — tiny fragments of slowly decomposing plant or animal material that may accumulate over time in both marine and freshwater aquariums

Diadema (ˌdīə'dēmə) — long-spined sea urchins, found in all tropical seas; the often poisonous spines are directed toward the source of any disturbance

diaphragm — 1) a sheet of muscle separating the pulmonary and abdominal cavities of terrestrial vertebrates; 2) the bellows of an aquarium air pump, usually made of synthetic rubber and requiring periodic replacement

diatom — any of the golden brown protists, also called stramenopiles, freshwater or marine, that produce a bivalved shell composed of silicon dioxide

diatom filter — a device for clearing fine particulate matter from aquarium water, employing diatomaecous earth as the medium

diatom filter

diatomaceous earth (¦dīəd·ə¦māshəs ərth) — a mineral deposit comprised of the shells of billions of fossil diatoms, often mined for use as an abrasive or filtration medium

dichotomus — having only two possible paths or choices; taxonomic references often employ "keys" constructed to allow identification of an organism by a logical process of elimination

dichromism — the property of having two distinct color phases or forms, often distinguishing the male and female of a species

Dictyota (¸diktē'ōd·ə) — a macrophytic brown marine alga found in shallow tropical waters and producing a series of flattened branches that repeatedly divide

diel — of the day, as in a "diel cycle" of behavior that recurs over a 24-hour period

dimorphic polyps ((')dī¸mórfik 'päləps) — some colonial hydrozoans in which the colony is composed of two distinct types of individuals that are nevertheless genetically identical

dinoflagellate (¦dīnōflə'jelāt) — protists of the Phylum Sarcomastigophora, characteristically bearing two locomotory flagella, each lying in a groove around the body, one perpendicular to the other; certain species are important to aquarists as fish parasites (*Amyloodinium*) and as the

zooxanthellae (*Gymnodinium*) of various cnidarians

Diodon ('dīə¸dän) — porcupinefish, Family Diodontidae, with spiny skins and the ability to ingest water or air to inflate themselves, making them difficult for a predator to swallow

dioecious ((')dī¦eshəs) — referring to flowering plants in which both male and female flowers are borne on separate individuals (*see* MONOECIOUS)

Discosoma (də'skó¸sōmə) — a genus of false corals, Phylum Cnidaria, Order Corallimorpharia, often imported for minireef aquariums

disinfectant — any agent that kills disease-producing organisms

Distichodus ('distə̇kədəs) — omnivorous characins from tropical Africa; infrequently available in the aquarium trade

dither fish — those placed in the same aquarium with a potential breeding pair to encourage the latter to spawn by giving them a sense of security necessary for successful parenting; may also serve as a "target" for the displacement of aggressive behavior between a potential breeding pair

diverticula (dīvə(r)¸tikyə'lə) — outpouchings, usually of the gut, but of any internal organ of an animal

Dolabrifera (dō'labrə¸fəra) — sea cats, opisthobranch gastropods with an internal shell, included in marine aquariums for algae control

dolomite — a natural carbonate mineral often recommended as a marine aquarium substrate in older references; it is not as satisfactory as other materials

Doras ('dōrəs) — one of the many genera of talking catfish, Family Doradidae, South American spiny catfish known for their ability to produce audible sounds

Dormitator ('dόrmē'tātər) — sleeper gobies inhabiting fresh to brackish waters

dorsal — anatomical reference to the back; in vertebrates the spinal cord is in this position

dorsal fin — the appendage, sometimes consisting of both spinous and nonspinous sections, arising from the midline of the back of all fish

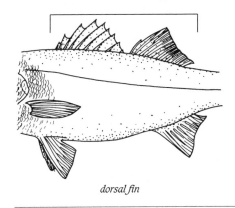

dorsal fin

dorsal spines — the supporting elements of the spinous portion of the dorsal fin

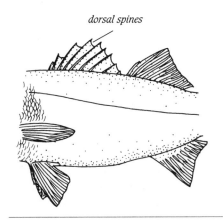

dorsal spines

dottyback — any of the small sea basses in the genus *Pseudochromis*

dragonet — any of the marine fish of Family Callyonimidae; the two most popular species are also known as "mandarinfish"

Dromia (‚drōmēə) — sponge crabs, a species from tropical waters that camouflages itself by attaching a piece of living sponge to its carapace

duckweed — any member of the genus *Lemna*, tiny flowering plants that float on the surface of freshwater ponds and aquariums

Dulaniella ('dü‚lən(y)ələ) — a genus of unicellular marine algae often cultured as a food source for other marine organisms

dulse ('dəls) — leafy red seaweeds, usually those harvested for food or animal feed; in the aquarium it is used for feeding herbivorous marine fish

Dutch-type aquarium — 1) one in which various species of freshwater aquatic plants, arranged in an artistic, naturalistic manner, are the primary aesthetic feature; 2) if marine, referring to a tank in which both invertebrates and fish are maintained, and filtration is accomplished by a wet/dry filtration system

dwarf angel — any of the marine fish of the genus *Centropyge*, mostly under 3 inches (7.6 cm) in length and feeding primarily on algae and tiny invertebrates

dwarf cichlid — any of the freshwater fish of the genus *Apistogramma*, together with related genera, seldom reaching over three inches (7.6 cm) in length and native to Central and South America

Echinaster (ə'kinästər) — a common sea star of the tropical Atlantic and West Indies often imported for the marine aquarium; predatory on bivalve mollusks and other sessile invertebrates

echinoderm (ə'kīnō,derm) — literally "spiny skin," any member of Phylum Echinodermata, exclusively marine invertebrates with radially symmetrical bodies and a water vascular system found in no other animal group

Echinodorus (ə'kīnō,dórəs) — Amazon sword plants, popular freshwater aquarium plants from North, Central, and South America producing a rosette of leaves and bearing flowers on a stalk extending above the water surface; under aquarium conditions, some regularly produce runners bearing plantlets

Echinometra (ə'kīnō,metrə) — rockdwelling sea urchins sometimes imported for algae control in the aquarium

echiurid (,ekē'yùrəd) — any of the wormlike marine invertebrates in the Phylum Echiurida, characterized by an eversible, flattened appendage used for capturing particulate food and commonly introduced into the marine aquarium with live rock

ecolabeling — a proposed system for categorization of species according to their relative adaptability to captive husbandry, designed with the goal of reducing the number of nonadaptable species collected for the aquarium trade

ecosystem — all of the physical and biological components of a specific geographic area and the interactions among them, usually defined by a dominant feature, such as a coral reef or lake

ecotype — a variety of a species that is characteristic of a particular ecosystem or habitat

ectoderm — the outer layer of embryonic tissue, giving rise to such structures as the skin and nervous system

ectoparasite — one attached to the outer body surface of the host organism

ectoparasite

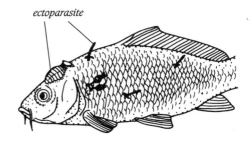

eelgrass — common name for the freshwater plants in the genus *Vallisneria*, and for the marine flowering plant *Zostera marinae*; either may be kept in an appropriate aquarium

Eichhornia ('īkə‚hórnēə) — water hyacinths; freshwater neotropical plants with long, pendant root systems and flotation structures at the bases of the leaves; a pest plant in some tropical habitats, though often grown in aquariums and especially in garden ponds for their attractive flower spikes

Eigenmannia ('īgən‚manēə) — glass knifefish, particularly *E. virescens* found in freshwater floodplains of tropical South America and sometimes imported for aquariums

elasmobranch (ə'lazmə‚braŋk) — any of the cartilaginous fish, including sharks, skates, and rays

electric shock organ — specialized structures possessed by some fish that permit them to generate a charge that ranges, depending upon the species, from millivolts to several hundred volts; such discharges are utilized for a variety of purposes from mate recognition to food capture to defense

electrolytes — solutions that conduct electricity

Electrophorus (ə‚lek'träf(ə)rəs) — the electric eel, *E. electricus*

element — a chemical substance composed of only one type of atoms and thus irreducible to components by ordinary chemical means

Eleocharis (‚elē'äkərə s) — spikerushes, sedge plants of wide distribution with extremely narrow, elongate leaves, often used for decorative effect in planted aquariums

Eleotris (¦elē¦ōtrəs) — sleeper gobies, Family Gobiidae, found in brackish water habitats

Ellisella (ə‚lisəl'ə) — marine gorgonian corals often with attractive coloration and frequently imported for the aquarium

Elodea (ə'lōdēə) — *E. densa*, often incorrectly called "*Anacharis*" in pet shops; this vining, dark green, bushy plant, usually sold in bunches, does best in cool, rather than tropical, aquariums or in a garden pond

emergent — said of leaves or flowers that are borne above the water surface by an otherwise aquatic plant

encrusting — forming a thin, usually hard layer on a solid substrate

endangered species — one recognized under law as so imperiled that a single event could render it extinct in the wild; also applied by ecologists to any species considered in peril of extinction, regardless of its legal status

endoderm — the inner embryonic tissue layer giving rise to such structures as the digestive and respiratory systems

endodermal — of or having to do with the endoderm

endoecism (¦en(,)dō¦əsizm) — a symbiotic relationship between two species in which one lives within the body of the other but does no harm to it

endoparasite — one that lives inside the body of the host organism

Entacmaea (ən·tək,māə) — bubble-tipped anemone, a host for many species of clownfish and the one most readily maintained under aquarium conditions

entoproct — any member of Phylum Entoprocta, small, colonial marine invertebrates that encrust solid substrates and feed by means of a specialized organ, the lophophore

enzymes — proteins that catalyze chemical reactions in living cells

Epalzeorhynchos ((')ēpəl'zēorīn,kōs) — the red-tailed and red-finned "sharks" of Southeast Asia, actually cyprinids; often included in freshwater community aquariums

epidermal — having to do with the epidermis, or outer layer of skin

Epiplatys (¦epə'platis) — egg-laying toothed carps of tropical Africa, with several strikingly colored species kept by killifish enthusiasts

epithelium (¦epə'th'ēlēəm) — a layer of tissue exposed to the environment, including the epidermis, but also including the linings of the alimentary tract and other internal surfaces; the latter often bears cilia and secretes mucus

epizoic — living upon the outer body surface of an animal, but doing no harm to it

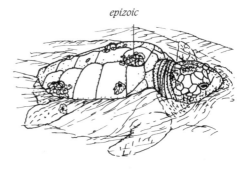

epizoic

Epsom salt — magnesium sulfate ($MgSO_4$), often combined with sodium chloride to produce a rudimentary form of synthetic seawater

Equetus ('e,kwētəs) — reef drums, usually black-and-white-striped marine fish regularly imported from Florida and the West Indies

erythromycin (ə,rithrə'mīsᵊn) — an antibiotic sometimes added to the marine aquarium for control of blue-green algae; it is extremely toxic to nitrifying bacteria

Erythropodium (ė¦rithrə,pōdēəm) — a soft coral with large, flowing polyps and a reddish colored, rubbery skeleton that grows over solid surfaces

Escenius ('esᵊnēus) — Indo-Pacific blennies, the most commonly imported species of which is *E. bicolor*, the orange and black bicolor blenny

esophagus — the tube leading from the mouth to the stomach

Esox ('ē,säks) — pikes, predatory fish of North American waters that hide among vegetation and ambush prey; often exhibited in large aquariums

esterified — having formed an ester, or chemical bond of the general form

$$-C-O-C-$$

estuary — an ecosystem formed where a river meets the ocean, and characterized by fluctuations in salinity due to tidal movement

Etroplus (ə̇.'troplǝs) — the only genus of cichlids found on the Indian subcontinent; popular with brackish-water aquarium enthusiasts

eucarids ((¦)yü¦kärids) — true shrimps, decapod crustaceans in several families, including numerous species regularly exhibited in marine aquariums

eukaryote ((¦)yü¦ka(a)rē,ōt) — a living organism comprised of cells having a distinct membrane-bound nucleus and other subcellular structures enclosed in membranes

Eunicea (yü'nī(,)sē) — photosynthetic gorgonian soft corals descriptively named "knobby candelabra"

euphausid ((,)yü,fȯzē,ə̇d) — krill, shrimplike marine crustaceans often sold in freeze-dried or frozen form as an aquarium food

Euphyllia (,yü,fil(y)ǝ) — stony corals, four species of which are popular with minireef enthusiasts because of their unusual tentacle shapes and ease of care

euthanasia (,yüthǝ'nāzh(ē)ǝ) — mercy killing, or the deliberate killing of an organism to spare it from pain or suffering

evolution — biological change resulting in the development of new species from ancestral species due to natural selection acting upon genetic variability in the latter

excreta (ek'skrēd·ǝ) — solid wastes produced by an animal; feces

excretion — the physiological process of waste elimination in cells or organisms

excurrent opening — one, as in mollusks, from which water flows out toward the environment

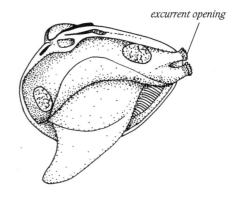

excurrent opening

exopthalmus (,ek,säf'thalmǝs) — a disorder of both marine and freshwater fish in which the eyeball protrudes noticeably from the eye socket, symptomatic of a variety of pathological conditions

external filter — any aquarium filter not located within the tank itself (*see* CANISTER FILTER, POWER FILTER, TRICKLE FILTER, WET/DRY FILTER)

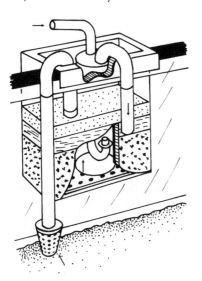

external filter

extinction — the loss of a species from its ecoystem

extratentacular ('ekstrə‚ten‧ˈtakyələ(r)) — literally, "outside the tentacles," referring to the process of daughter colony formation by certain species of stony corals, in which an offspring buds from the outer surface of the parent colony

eye — a multicellular organ sensitive to light

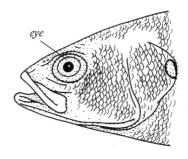

eye

eye stalk — the short appendage supporting the visual organs of many mollusks and crustaceans

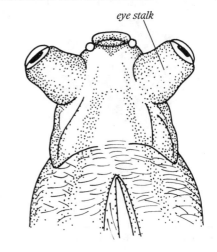

eye stalk

FAAS — Federation of American Aquarium Societies

family — a group of related genera

fanworm — any of the segmented worms of Families Sabellidae and Serpulidae possessing a feeding structure superficially resembling a fan, feather duster, or parasol, often imported for marine aquariums

fanworm

Farlowella ('fär,lō,wəla) — South American loricarid catfish with extremely elongated bodies

Favia ('fävēə) — a stony coral with individual corallites arranged like the cells of a honeycomb

Favites ('fävētəz) — a stony coral similar to, and frequently confused with, *Favia*

fertilizer — any material used as a source of nutrients for enhancement of plant growth

filamentous (¦filə¦mentəs) — having a threadlike structure, as with many freshwater and marine algae that grow in aquariums

filter — any device for maintaining the quality of aquarium water by removal of particulate or chemical substances, the accumulation of which would be harmful to the organisms exhibited in the tank

fireworm — one of several tropical polychaete annelids with venomous bristles capable of delivering a painful sting if the organism is carelessly handled

fishkeeping — an idiomatic reference to the aquarium hobby

flagellum (flə'jeləm) — in common usage, an elongate, whiplike structure employed for locomotion in several groups of unicellular organisms; cell biologists reserve this term only for prokaryotic cells

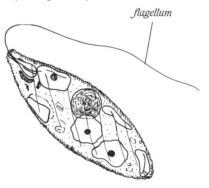

flagellum

flashing — a fish behavior characterized by rapid, glancing contact with a solid object in an effort to displace an external parasite or other irritation, so called because the light-colored underbelly of the fish is thus exposed to momentary view

flatworm — any member of Phylum Platyhelminthes, including the non-parasitic freshwater form, *Planaria*, and numerous parasites of marine and freshwater fish and invertebrates

flavins — yellow plant pigments thought to absorb blue light during photosynthesis

fluidized-bed filter — a device that accomplishes biological filtration through growth of nitrifying bacteria on a mass of sand or tiny spheres of synthetic materials suspended in a current of water passing though it; although similar in principle to other types of biological filtration systems, this method allows for maximum carrying capacity while minimizing the size of the filter itself

fluidized-bed filter

fluorescent tube — a lamp consisting of a long glass cylinder, coated on the inside with phosphorescent chemicals, sealed, and filled with gas, through which the passage of an electrical discharge results in light production

foam fractionation — a synonym for protein skimming

foam nest — an alternative name for the bubble nest constructed by labyrinth fish

Fontinalis ('fänt⁹nələs) — willow moss, freshwater mosses often cultivated in cold water aquariums

foot — the muscular, fleshy appendage of a mollusk, employed for moving upon, clinging to, or burrowing within a substrate

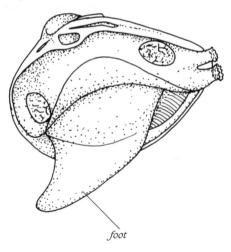

foot

foraminiferans (fə‚ramə'nif(ə)rəns) — members of a group of unicellular marine organisms that are important components of plankton; their distinctively shaped skeletal structures are useful to marine geologists investigating sedimentary deposits

Forcipiger ((')fȯ(r)ˌsipəgər) — long-snouted butterflyfish, Family Chaetodontidae, popular as aquarium subjects

formalin — a solution of formaldehyde gas in water, used as a preservative for taxonomic specimens and as a therapeutic agent in the treatment of ectoparasite infestations in both marine and freshwater fish

fossorial — adapted for digging or burrowing

freshwater — water of low salinity, lacking significant amounts of the anions flouride, chloride, bromide, and iodide

Fromia (f(r)ōmēə) — small sea stars popular with minireef enthusiasts

because of their bright coloration and nonpredatory habits

fry — recently hatched fish

Fundulus ('fəndəˌləs) — studfish, Family Fundulidae, native to North and Central America and often maintained in temperate aquariums because the males are colorful

fungicide — any agent that kills fungi

fungus — plural: fungi; nonphotosynthetic eukaryotes that feed via extracellular digestion, sometimes pathogenic

G

Galaxea (gā͵laksēə) — a stony coral characterized by massive, usually dome-shaped colonies with individual corallites forming raised bumps on the surface

Gambusia (gam'byüzh(ē)ə) — mosquito fish, Family Poecilidae, *G. affinis*, native to the southeastern United States, is the best known and is widely introduced for mosquito control; other species are endangered

ganoid scale — the thick, enamel-like epidermal structures of gars, sturgeons, and related fish

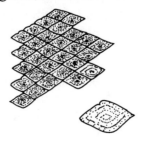

ganoid scale

Gasterosteus (͵gastərō'stē͵us) — sticklebacks, brackish-water and freshwater fish of North America and Europe that are often maintained in specialized aquariums

gastropod (͵gastrō·päd) — a snail or mollusk with a univalve shell and in which the developing larva undergoes twisting, or torsion, resulting in the juxtapositioning of anterior and posterior ends of the alimentary tract

gastrotrich ('gastrə·͵trik) — microscopic freshwater invertebrates, characterized by a series of bristles on the posterior portion of the body; often a food source for fish fry or larger invertebrates

Gelbstoff — literally, "yellow matter" in German, a term coined to refer collectively to the organic compounds that produce yellowing of aquarium waters, both fresh and marine

gene — a unit of DNA that codes for a single protein molecule

gene flow — the movement of genetic information between two populations of a species as a result of crossbreeding

gene pool — the total amount of genetic diversity within a species

genital papilla ('jenəd·ᵊl pa'pilə) — a tube extending from the urogenital opening, used for egg or sperm deposition; typically found in fish that attach their eggs to a solid object

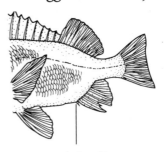

genital papilla

genus — plural: genera; a group of closely related species

Geophagus ((')jē¦äfəgəs) — "earth eater," South American cichlids that feed by taking substrate material into the mouth and expelling it through the gill covers to obtain burrowing organisms

GH — abbreviation for "general hardness" or the total amount of dissolved salts of calcium and magnesium present in a sample of water

gill — the anatomical structure in some aquatic organisms that permits gas exchange across the walls of capillaries between the bloodstream and the surrounding water

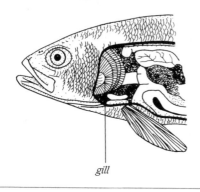

gill

gill cover — the opercle, or flap, that protects the gills of fish

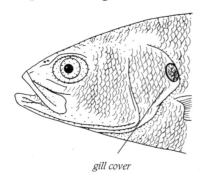

gill cover

gill filaments — in fish, the smallest subdivisions of the gills

gill raker — structures that support and give rise to the gill filaments of fish

Gingylostoma (ˌjiŋglə'mästəmə) — nurse sharks, so named because of the sucking sound they make when feeding

glutinant — any substance that causes the clumping of small particles to form a jellylike mass

Gnathonemus ('näthəˌnēməs) — elephant nose fish, Family Mormyridae, from the Congo River, Africa

Gobiodon ('gōbēˌdən) — coral gobies, tropical marine fish from the Indo-Pacific region living among the branches of various hard and soft corals

Gobiosoma ('gōbēˌsōma) — sharpnosed gobies, fish from the tropical Atlantic and Caribbean, including the neon goby, *G. oceanops*, and other popular aquarium species; several can be commercially produced through aquaculture

Gobius ('gōbēəs) — type genus of Family Gobiidae, characteristically with the pelvic fins fused to form a suckerlike appendage for holding onto solid surfaces

Goniastrea (ˌgōnē¦astrēə) — a stony coral, Family Faviidae, with large, hexagonal corallites forming a hemispherical colony

Goniopora ('gōnēə,pōrə) — poritid stony corals with large, elongate flowerlike polyps, often imported but seldom successfully adapted to aquarium care

Gorgonia (gȯr(r)'gōnēə) — sea fans, gorgonian soft corals in which the body branches are repeatedly fused to form a network

gorgonian (('·)gȯ(r)'gōnēən) — any of the eight-tentacled anthozoans producing an axial skeleton covered by a usually colorful outer tissue layer that gives rise to the polyps

gorgonin ('gȯ(r)gənə̇n) — the structural protein comprising the axial skeleton of a gorgonian

gourami (gü'rämē) — labyrinth fish in several genera characterized by modification of the pectoral fins into sensory "feelers"

Gracillaria (,grasə'la(a)rēə) — a macrophytic red marine alga often cultivated as fish food and for display

Gramma ('gramə) — small sea basses of the tropical Atlantic and Caribbean frequently kept in aquariums because of their bright coloration, nonaggressive temperament, and hardiness

gravel — pieces of rock ranging in size from $^1/_{16}$ to $^1/_4$ inch (1.6 to 6.3 mm) in diameter

ground fault circuit interrupter (GFCI) — an electrical device that compares the current flowing on one side of a circuit with that flowing on the opposite side, and that opens the circuit to prevent personal injury when a difference greater than a few milliamps is detected

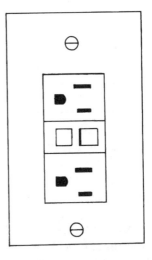

ground fault circuit interrupter (GFCI)

grounding — providing a path for electricity to travel into the earth, usually to eliminate an unwanted charge or to protect personnel from injury by providing a path of least resistance for current flow

guanin ('gwä,nən) — a substance in the scales of fish giving them an iridescent sheen

Gyrinocheilus (jə̇rinō,kēləs) — algae-eating freshwater fish from Asia that as adults may also attack other fish housed in the same aquarium

habitat — the geographic locality, together with its biological components, in which a species is typically found

Halichoeres (ˌhaləˈkirəs) — marine wrasses, Family Labridae, many species of which are adaptable to aquarium care

Halimeda (ˌhaləˈmēdə) — a macrophytic green marine alga with a calcified skeleton consisting of flattened plates or disks attached to each other at the edges

Haplochalaena (ˈha(ˌ)plōˌkalānə) — the blue-ringed octopus, a species sometimes imported, but that should be avoided by aquarists because of the toxic venom delivered by its deadly bite

Haplochromis (ˈha(ˌ)plōˌkrōməs) — one of many genera of cichlids found in the rift lakes of eastern Africa

hard water — water that contains dissolved salts of calcium and magnesium in a concentration greater than 200 parts per million

hatchling — any organism that has recently emerged from the egg

hawkfish — marine fish, Family Cirrhitidae, that characteristically perch atop a coral head or other prominence to watch for prey; many are popular aquarium fish

head — the anterior portion of a bilaterally symmetrical animal, bearing sense organs such as eyes or antennae, and enclosing the brain

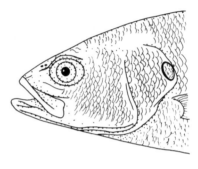

head

head-and-lateral-line erosion (HLLE) — a condition observed in some marine and freshwater fish, notably those in Families Acanthuridae, Pomacanthidae, Pomacentridae, and Chiclidae, but not restricted to these, in which the scales and epidermis of the face and along the lateral line erode away, leaving depigmented areas that may become infected; while the exact cause is unknown, studies suggest that the condition is associated with deficiencies of vitamins C or A or both

head-and-lateral-line erosion (HLLE)

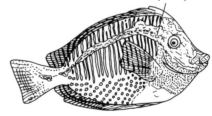

Heliofungia (¦hēlēō¸fənjēə) — plate coral, a stony coral with a rounded, biscuit-shaped skeleton and long tentacles often tipped in pink; it is a bottom-dwelling species capable of slow movement across the substrate and sometimes confused with a sea anemone; difficult to maintain unless provided with bright illumination and appropriate water conditions

Heliopora (¦helēō¸pórə) — blue coral, the monospecific genus of the anthozoan Order Coenothecalia, usually displayed in the aquarium as a dead skeleton, which is light blue in color

Hemiancistrus ('hēmēə¸an'sistrəs) — South American suckermouth catfish useful for algae control in the aquarium

Hemichromis (¦hemē¸krōməs) — jewel cichlids, colorful West African species that are highly territorial and aggressive, but often maintained in aquariums

Hemigrammus (¦hemē¸graməs) — South American characins of which numerous species are good community aquarium fish

Heniochus (henēō¸kəs) — pennant butterflyfish, found in the Indo-Pacific and, unlike other members of their family, living in schools and feeding upon planktonic organisms in midwater

Hepatus (¦hepətəs) — box crabs with a pale-colored carapace bearing bright maroon blotches; they have chelae adapted for feeding on snails and are often exhibited

herbivore — any organism that has living plant matter as its primary diet

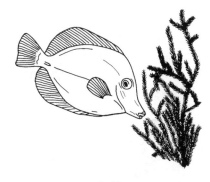

herbivore

hermaphroditism (he(r)'mafrə¸dīd·¸izəm) — a condition in which a single individual possesses both male and female reproductive organs, either simultaneously or at different stages in its life cycle

hermatypic (¸hə(r)'me'tipik) — corals that contain symbiotic dinoflagellates known as "zooxanthellae"

Heros ('hē(¸)rōz) — South American cichlids, especially the severum, *H. severum*

Herpolitha (¸hərpə'lithə) — slipper coral, a bottom-dwelling, mobile stony coral with an elongated skeleton rounded on either end

Heteractis (¦hed·ə¦rāktis) — tropical anemones of the Indo-Pacific, at least three of which are host to anemonefish; they are often kept in aquariums although they are difficult to maintain successfully

Heterandria (¦hed·ə¦randrēə) — small, live bearing fish from the coastal southeastern United States, including the least killifish, *H. formosa*, the smallest North American vertebrate

Heteranthera (¦hed·ə·'ran(t)thərə) — a pondweed of tropical and subtropical America, cultivated for its kidney-shaped floating leaves

heterocercal ('hed·ərō͵serkəl) — a type of caudal fin found in primitive fish, including gars, sturgeons, sharks, paddlefish, and bowfins, in which the upper lobe arises from the upturned terminal vertebrae, and the lower lobe from the ventral portions of the same bones

heterocercal

heterotroph ('hed·ərō·͵träf) — any organism that obtains energy by consuming preformed food molecules

heterotrophic (¦hed·ərō·¦trōfik) — of or having to do with a heterotroph or its mode of nutrition

hexacoral (͵heksə'kərəl) — a colonial anthozoan with tentacles in multiples of six

hinge ligament — the tough, flexible tissue that secures the two shells of a bivalve mollusk at the area where they rotate against each other

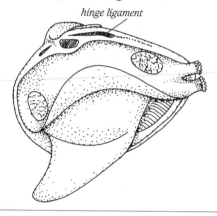

hinge ligament

Hippocampus ('hi(͵)pō'kampəs) — seahorses, comprised of some 30 species distributed worldwide in shallow seas

Hippopus (͵hipə'pús) — a monospecific genus of giant clams, regularly produced by aquaculture and maintained in minireef aquariums

holdfast — any structure produced by a sessile organism for the purpose of anchoring it to a solid substrate

holdfast

Holocanthus (¦hälō'kan(t)thəs) — large marine angelfish of the tropical Atlantic and Caribbean

holothurid (¸hälō'thürəd) — a sea cucumber, Phylum Echinodermata, Class Holothuroidea

homeothermic (hō¦mói(y)ə¦thər mik) — referring to an organism with the ability to maintain a constant internal body temperature; warm-blooded

homocercal — the type of caudal fin found in most bony fishes, in which the vertebral column terminates at the fin base

homogeneity — uniformity; in biology, usually referring to a lack of variation among the individuals comprising a population

hood — an enclosure housing light fixtures for aquarium illumination, usually incorporating a cover for the entire tank

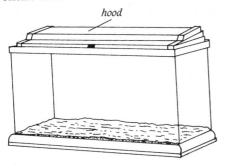

hood

Hoplolatilus (¸häplō¸läd·ət'ləs) — sand tilefish, Family Malacanthidae, some species of which are small enough to be accommodated in a suitable aquarium

Hoplosternum (¸häplō¦stərnəm) — South American armored catfish often confused with *Corydoras*, which they closely resemble

hybrid — the offspring resulting from crossbreeding between two different species

hybridization (¸hībrədə'zāshən) — the process of hybrid formation, either in nature or the deliberate crossing by human intervention of two species in an effort to produce offspring with a combination of parental traits

Hydnophora (¦hīdnō¦forə) — horn coral, a stony coral, usually bright green, popular with reef aquarists because of the ease of propagation

Hydra ('hīdrə) — a freshwater hydrozoan resembling a tiny sea anemone that is sometimes a problem in breeding aquariums because of its ability to catch and eat fish fry

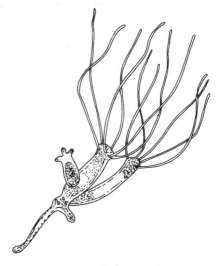

Hydra

Hydrocotyle ('hī(ˌ)drō'käd·ᵊlē) — water pennywort, a low, creeping aquatic or bog plant bearing rounded leaves with scalloped edges

hydrogen ion — (H⁺) a hydrogen atom that has lost its electron, the concentration of which determines the pH of a solution

hydrogen peroxide — (H₂O₂) a compound sometimes added to aquarium water to increase the oxygen content as it dissociates rapidly into water and free oxygen; also used as a disinfectant for treating wounds in fish

hydroid ('hī,dróyd) — any member of the cnidarian Class Hydrozoa, but most often applied to the flowerlike polyp form of these organisms

hydromedusa ('hīdrə,mə'd(y)üsə) — the free-swimming stage in the life cycle of a hydrozoan, shaped like a bell or umbrella and superficially resembling a sea jelly

hydrometer — a device for measuring specific gravity

hydrophilic ('hīdrə¦filik) — literally "water loving," said of substances, such as salts, that readily dissolve in or mix with water

hydrophobic ('hīdrə¦fōbik) — literally "water fearing," said of substances, such as oils, that do not readily dissolve in or mix with water

hydroxyl (hī'dräksəl) — a hydroxide ion, OH⁺, formed when a water molecule dissociates

hydrozoan (ˌhīdrə'zōen) — any member of the cnidarian Class Hydrozoa, characterized by a life cycle exhibiting alternation between a polyp stage and a medusa stage

Hygrophila (hī'gräfilə) — freshwater flowering plants of the *Acanthus* family sold as bunches of rooted cuttings, of rapid growth under aquarium conditions

Hyphessobrycon (hī,fesə'brī,kän) — a large genus of small South American characins including some of the most popular species for freshwater community aquariums, such as the bleeding heart tetra

hypochlorite (hī(ˌ)pō,klōr,īt) — an ion formed from chlorine and oxygen that is a strong oxidizer; household bleach, sodium hypochlorite, is used as a sterilizing agent in various aquarium-related applications

Hypostomus ((')hi¦pästəməs) — suckermouth catfish from South America, often maintained in freshwater aquairums for control of algae growth

Hypseleotris ('hipsə,lēə,trəs) — gudgeons, Family Gobiidae, from Australia and New Zealand

Hypsypops ('hipsə,päps) — the Garibaldi damselfish, *H. rubicunda*, still sometimes seen in aquarium shops, despite its legal status as a protected species and requirement for cool water; it is found off the California coast and lives in kelp forests

I

ich ('ik) — an infestation of the skin of a freshwater fish by the ciliated protozoan parasite *Ichthyophthirius multifillis*

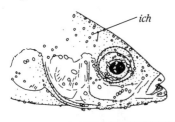

ichthyologist ('iktheə'äləjəst) — a biologist who specializes in the study of fish

ichthyology ('ikthēə'äləjē) — the branch of biological science concerned with the morphology, physiology, taxonomy, and ecology of fish

Ichthyophonus ('ikthēə'äfōn,əs) — a microscopic fungus that sometimes infests captive marine fish; it is incurable

Ichthyopthirius (,ikthēäp'thirēəs) — ciliated protozoan parasites of freshwater aquarium fish; *I. multifillis* is the organism responsible for the disease ich

Ichthyopthirius

ick — alternate spelling for "ich"

Ictalurus (,iktə'lúrəs) — North American catfish, including the channel catfish, often kept by freshwater hobbyists and raised for human consumption

illicium (ə'lis(h)ēəm) — the "fishing pole" of angler- or frogfish, formed from the first dorsal fin spine

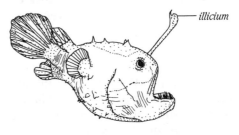

illuminance — the amount of light falling upon a given area

immersion heater — an electrical device for raising the temperature of an aquarium, consisting of a metallic element controlled by a thermostat and enclosed in a glass or metal tube to prevent contact with water

immersion heater

75

impeller — a series of paddles arranged around a shaft or axle, the spinning of which pushes water through the volute of a pump

incisor — the chisel-like front teeth of some vertebrates, including many fish, used for cutting food

Indo-Pacific — the region of the sea including both the Indian and Pacific Oceans, or referring to any species or feature of this region

infauna (ən'fónə) — collectively, the organisms inhabiting the interior of an object, such as a porous rock or wooden dock piling, or between the grains of an aggregate, such as sand or gravel

infusoria (,infyə'zōrēə) — microscopic organisms, often ciliated protists and rotifers cultured as a food for freshwater fish fry

insoluble — not dissolvable; unable to form a solution with water or another solute

inhalant siphon — a body opening, such as in mollusks, through which water flows in from the environment

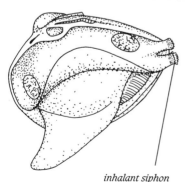

inhalant siphon

instar — a larval stage of a crustacean, each associated with a molt

interorbital width — the distance between the nearest edges of the eyes, measured across the top of the head of a fish

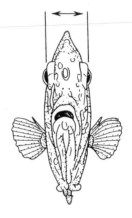

interorbital width

intestine — the portion of the alimentary tract where food is digested and nutrients absorbed

iodine — a chemical element (I) present in seawater at approximately 0.6 parts per million, and essential for certain marine organisms

ion — an atom or molecule with a net electrical charge resulting from the gain or loss of electrons

ion exchanger — a synthetic resin able to sequester certain elements or compounds from water by swapping them for another, usually sodium; sometimes utilized to purify water for aquarium use

iron — a chemical element (Fe) required in trace amounts by many organisms, and frequently added to aquariums for the benefit of plants or seaweeds

irradiance — the amount of light energy falling on a given area

Isaurus (ī'sórəs) — Indo-Pacific colonial anthozoans of the Order Zoantharia, often maintained in marine aquariums

Isochrysis (ˌī(ˌ)sōˌkrīsəs) — a unicellular marine alga often cultured as a food for certain other organisms, such as rotifers intended for feeding to fish larvae

isthmus (ist(h)ˌməs) — a narrow subregion of a fish's trunk, interposed between the gill flaps

J–K

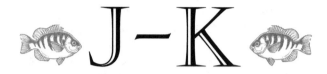

jawfish — any species in the Family Opisthognathidae; these marine fish have large mouths and typically burrow into the substrate; the most commonly seen aquarium species is *Opisthognathus aurifrons*, from the tropical Atlantic and Caribbean

jawless fish — any of the Class Agnatha, primitive forms such as lampreys and hagfish; seldom exhibited in aquariums

jellyfish — a sea jelly, or schyphozoan cnidarian

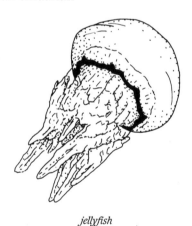

jellyfish

Julidochromis (jü¦lēdō₁krōməs) — cichlids of Lake Tanganyika, Africa, many species of which are popular with hobbyists

Kalkwasser — literally, "chalk water," German for limewater, a solution of calcium hydroxide added to marine reef aquariums as a source of calcium ions

KH — "German hardness," a scale of measurement of alkalinity or carbonate hardness (*see* APPENDIX 1: MEASUREMENTS, EQUIVALENTS, AND FORMULAS)

killifish — egg-laying fish in the Families Cyprinodontidae, Fundulidae, and Rivulidae, from temperate, tropical, and subtropical areas of North America, South America, and Africa; they are the focus of interest for a substantial number of specialized aquarium hobbyists

kinorhynch ('kinə₁riŋ) — marine invertebrates, microscopic in size or nearly so, that are a component of the fauna of live sand and live rock

koi ('kȯi) — the common carp, *Cyprinis carpio*, cultivated for centuries in the Far East and more recently in Europe and the Western Hemisphere in garden ponds; they are notable for their vivid color patterns

krill — any euphausid crustacean, but often *Euphausia superba*, harvested from the sea and sold in frozen or freeze-dried form as a food for aquarium fish

L

Labeo (ˌlabēō) — freshwater "sharks," actually cyprinids, from Southeast Asia and Africa, frequently included in freshwater community tanks; larger specimens can become aggressive

Labidochromis (ˌlabēdōˌkrōməs) — one of the many genera of cichlids of Lake Malawi, Africa

Labroides ('lāˌbro(y)dəs) — cleaner wrasses, Family Labridae, found in the Indo-Pacific and often imported for the aquarium because of their habit of removing parasites from other fish; only one species, *L. dimidiatus*, adapts well to captivity

labyrinth fish — any of the Family Anabantidae, freshwater fish of tropical Africa and the Asian subcontinent characterized by a specialized organ that permits them to breathe atmospheric air

Lactoria ('lakˌtorēə) — cowfish, marine species of the boxfish family, Ostraciidae, with prominent "horns" protruding above the eyes; slow moving, they graze upon tiny invertebrates

lacustrine (ləˈkəstrən) — lake-dwelling, or having to do with the environment within a lake

Lagarosiphon (ˌlāgə(r)ōˈsīfən) — graceful, green bunch plants from Madagascar, including *L. madagascarensis*, resembling *Elodea*, but preferring warmer water

Lagenandra (ˌlajəˌna(a)ndrə) — aquatic plants of the *Arum* family, native to swamps of the Indian subcontinent; they form upright rosettes of thick, shiny leaves arising from a rhizome

laminar — of or having to do with a layered structure, especially of currents flowing within a body of water or air

Lamprologus (ˌlamˈprəˌlōgəs) — one of the numerous genera of cichlids of Lake Tanganyika, including many species popular with aquarium enthusiasts

lancefish — any of several small marine species harvested and sold, usually frozen, for feeding predatory aquarium fish

lancelet — a member of Phlyum Cephalochordata, primitive, fishlike marine invertebrates that live in sand and feed on smaller organisms; they are sometimes discovered in aquariums that contain a live sand bed

larva — an immature form of an invertebrate or fish that develops from the fertilized egg and changes into the adult form after a period of growth and development

lateral line — a structure lying, typically, along the middle of either side of the body of teleost fish, together with interconnected structures in the head; it senses changes in water pressure, permitting the fish to precisely control its swimming

lateral line

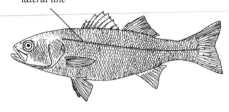

lateral line scale count — the number of scales from the first pored scale behind the gill opening to the base of the caudal fin; in species without a developed lateral line, the number of scales along the same approximate course

lateral line scale count

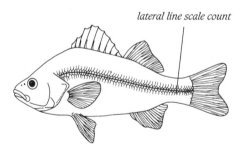

Lebrunia (ˌleˈbrün(y)ēə) — the antler anemone, an anthozoan of Florida and the Caribbean characterized by two types of tentacles, one resembling the antlers of a deer; although beautiful, it can deliver a painful sting

Leinardella (ˌlī'ən'ardələ) — large marine wrasses; the only species

frequently imported is *L. fasciata*, the harlequin tusk fish, boldly striped in red and white, with blue teeth

Lemna ('ləmnə) — tiny, floating flowering plants known as "duckweeds" often cultivated in freshwater aquariums and garden ponds

Lemnalia ('ləmnəlēə) — a thinly branched, arborescent soft coral without visible skeletal elements, commonly called "spaghetti coral"

Lepomis (lə'pōmə̇s) — North American centrarchids, the sunfish; sometimes maintained in aquariums by enthusiasts specializing in species native to that continent

Leporinus (ˌlepə'rēnəs) — herbivorous, elongate characins of the Amazon Basin; commonly seen species bear striking vertical bars

Leptogorgia ('leptəˌgōrjēə) — sea whips, gorgonian anthozoans often found in areas of lowered salinity, and sometimes maintained successfully in marine aquariums; they are more common in temperate than tropical waters

light spectrum — electromagnetic radiation with a wavelength between 100 and 1000 nanometers, including ultraviolet, visible, and infrared light; also a graphic representation of such radiation

limestone — rock formed by deposition of calcium carbonate in marine sediments; it occurs in many forms worldwide and is often used for decoration in marine aquariums and those designed for African rift lake cichlids

limewater — a saturated solution of calcium hydroxide often added to marine reef aquariums as a source of calcium ions (*see* KALKWASSER)

limewood — the product of a citrus tree, used for making aquarium air diffusers because of its porosity

Limia ('limēə) — file shells, bivalve marine mollusks often maintained in aquariums because of the bright red mantle; they require large amounts of planktonic food organisms

Limnophila ('limnō,filə) — vining aquatic flowering plants of the snapdragon family ranging from tropical Africa to Australia; commonly cultivated in aquariums for their light green, finely divided foliage; often incorrectly called "*Ambulia*"

Linckia ('linkēə) — sea stars, typically with smooth, rounded arms; often kept in marine aquariums for their bright blue, lavender and purple coloration, though somewhat challenging to maintain successfully

lionfish — any fish of the genera *Dendrochirus* or *Pterois*, but often applied only to *P. volitans*

Liopropoma (,lī'ō,prō'pōmə) — miniature sea basses, Family Serranidae, generally found only in deep water; though expensive, they are sought after by aquarists

because of their bright coloration and hardiness

Litophyton ('līd·ō'fītən) — soft corals from the Indo-Pacific that are popular with marine reef hobbyists because of the ease of propagation

live-bearer — any of the fish in Family Poecillidae, including many popular aquarium species such as the guppy, platy, swordtail, and molly, that give birth to live young

loach — elongate, bottom-dwelling fish from Southeast Asia that are often included in freshwater community aquariums; although they resemble catfish, they are members of the carp family

loam — soil containing a mixture of sand, clay and organic matter in varying proportions; generally considered ideal for the growth of a wide variety of plants, including aquatic species

Lobelia (lō'bel(y)ēə) — North American terrestrial or marsh plants; some are suitable for cultivation in garden ponds and bear tall spikes of either bright red or blue flowers in late summer

Lobophyllia (lō'bə'filēə) — a stony coral with large polyps that is adapted to living on the sea bottom in shallow water; it is often included in marine reef aquariums

Lobophytum (lō'be,fīdəm) — a soft coral with lobed branches, known as "devil's hand" or "leather finger coral"

longevity — the length of time an organism can reasonably be expected to live

longitudinal fission — lengthwise splitting, a mode of asexual reproduction exhibited in certain anthozoans and other invertebrate groups

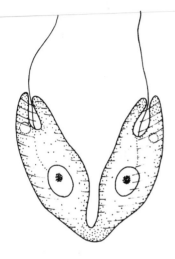

longitudinal fission

Loricaria (ˌlòrə'ka(a)rēə) — South American catfish, Family Loricariidae, with suckerlike mouths

Ludwigia (ləd'wigēə) — semiaquatic flowering plants, Family Onagraceae, of the southeastern United States and Central America, with upright stems bearing short, lance-shaped leaves, sometimes red in color

Lugol's solution — a solution of iodine and potassium iodide added to marine aquariums as a source of iodide ions; also used in greater concentration as a disinfectant for living coral specimens

lumen — anatomically, the opening within a tubulur structure, such as an intestine or blood vessel; in physics, a unit of measure of light energy

Lutjanus (lü'chānəs) — snappers, marine fish of Family Lutjanidae; harvested for table fare, smaller specimens are often kept in large aquariums

lux — a unit of irradiance equivalent to one lumen per square meter

Lybia (lī'bēə) — marine crabs of aquarium interest because of their habit of carrying small sea anemones that are used as mops to collect particulate food and that may also be brandished in defense

lymphocystis (ˌlim(p)fəˌsistəs) — a disease of marine fish caused by a virus and equivalent to a wart, characterized by the formation of a grayish white, irregular growth anywhere on the body but especially on the fins; treatable only with antiviral drugs

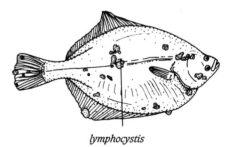

lymphocystis

Lysimachia (ˌlīsə'makēə) — moneywort or creeping Jenny, *L. nummularia* is a creeping plant of marshy areas with small, rounded, yellow leaves; a member of the primrose family

Lysmata (ˌlīsə'mātə) — marine shrimps frequently collected for the aquarium and popular with hobbyists because of their red coloration, sociability, and cleaning behavior

Lytechinus (ˌlī'tekinəs) — a sea urchin found in seagrass beds that often carries bits of debris that serves as camouflage

MAC — Marine Aquarium Council, an international nonprofit organization established to create a certification system for ornamental marine fish captured via sustainable techniques and held and handled under the best management practices

macroalgae — one of larger than microscopic size; to aquarists, any seaweed with a noninvasive growth habit exhibited in a marine aquarium

Macrodactyla (ˌmakrōˌdakˌtilə) — Indo-Pacific sea anemone often collected and exhibited as a host for clownfish; it is generally hardy in the aquarium

Macropharyngodon (ˌmakrōˌfəˌriŋ ˌgäden) — marine wrasses, Family Labridae, often collected because of their bright coloration, but seldom successfully adapted to the aquarium because of their specialized feeding habits

Macropodus ((ˈ)maˈkräˌpōdəs) — paradise fish, anabantids notable for beautiful coloration and often pugnacious behavior; they are more tolerant of cool temperatures than other members of the family

macrosymbiont (ˈmakrōˌsimbēˌänt) — the larger organism in a relationship in which two species are characteristically found in each other's presence

madreporite (ˈmadrəˌporīt) — the external opening of the water vascular system of echinoderms

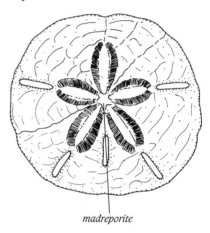

madreporite

magnesium — a chemical element (Mg) present in seawater at a concentration of 1290 parts per million; its carbonate salts comprise a portion of the hardness value of fresh water

mandible — in invertebrates, any movable jaw element; in vertebrates, only the lower jaw

mandibulate — said of invertebrates possessing mandibles

manganese — a chemical element (Mn) important to marine aquarists primarily as a trace component of seawater

Manicina (ˈmanəˌsēnə) — rose coral, a large-polyped scleractinian adapted for lying on the bottom in sand, mud, or gravel; found in Florida and the Caribbean

mantle — the fleshy structure enclosing the body of a mollusk; it secretes the shell

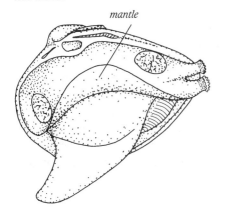

mantle

manubrium — a tubelike extension of the digestive cavity of cnidarian medusae that hangs from the center of the umbrella and is often lobed or frilled

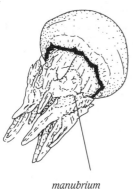

manubrium

marginal tentacles — thin projections from the outer edge of the mantle in certain mollusks, such as scallops

mariculture — captive propagation of marine organisms, usually on a commercial basis, by sexual or asexual methods

marine life — collective term for all species of organisms exhibited in aquariums devoted to oceanic habitats

marsh — an area characterized by the seasonal presence of shallow standing water but in which peat does not form (*see* BOG)

Marsilea (mär'silē ə) — water clover, freshwater ferns maintained in ponds and aquariums and having four lobed leaves resembling terrestrial clover

MASNA — Marine Aquarium Societies of North America, a confederation of hobbyist clubs focused on saltwater aquariums; it sanctions MACNA, the annual Marine Aquarium Conference of North America

Mastacembelus ('mastə,sembē,ləs) — spiny eels, Family Mastacembelidae, elongate, flattened fresh and brackish-water predatory fish from Southeast Asia, India, and China that make good aquarium inhabitants

maxillary — the upper jawbone in the skull of a fish, often bearing teeth

mbuna (em'bu̇nə) — common name, derived from the local word, for many of the cichlid fish of the rift lakes of East Africa, especially Lake Malawi

mechanical filtration — any method of water purification primarily intended to remove particulate matter by passing water over a medium such as floss, foam, or diatomaceous earth

medusa — a stage in the life cycle of certain cnidarians, and the dominant one in sea jellies, with the body characteristically shaped like a bell; they are able to swim by rhythmic pulsations

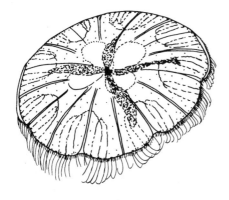

medusa

megavertebrate — any large species, such as a whale, elephant, or shark, as distinct from smaller ones, such as shrews, bats, or gobies

Meiacanthus ('mē(y)ə,kan(t)thəs) — fanged blennies, Family Blennidae, of the Indo-Pacific; several species are imported for aquariums

Melanochromis ('melənō,krōməs) — another of the numerous genera of cichlids endemic to Lake Malawi, Africa

melanophores ('melənə,fō(ə)rs) — cellular structures containing pigment molecules, found in vertebrate and invertebrate groups

Melanotaenia (melənō¦tēnēə) — rainbowfish, native to Australia and New Guinea, and popular as specialized subjects for a freshwater aquarium

membrane — any thin, resilient, sheetlike structure; biologically, the semipermeable double layer of lipid molecules and proteins enclosing a living cell or subcellular component

mercury vapor lamp — a high-intensity lighting device, operated by electricity, sometimes used for aquarium lighting when bright illumination is desired

mesenteries — tissues that suspend the internal organs of an animal within the body cavity

mesoderm — the middle layer of embryonic tissues, giving rise to such structures as the heart and muscles

mesogloea (mezō'glēə) — undifferentiated, jellylike material comprising much of the body structure of cnidarians and ctenophores

metabolism — the process of deriving energy from food molecules by a living cell or organism

metabolite — any substance acted upon during the process of metabolism

metal halide lamp — a high-intensity device, operated by electricity, utilized as an aquarium light source when very bright light is needed, as with a miniature reef aquarium or freshwater plant tank

metamerism (mȧtȧ͵mȧrizȧm) — segmentation, the repetition of body parts in animals such as annelids and crustaceans

metamorphosis — the process of transformation of a larval form into an adult

methylene blue ('methȧ͵lēn blü) — a chemical dye sometimes used as an aquarium medication or disinfectant; it must be employed with caution as it is toxic to nitrifying bacteria

Metynnis ('mȧd·ȧ͵nes) — South American tetras of herbivorous habits, related to piranhas and pacus

microalgae — any small, though not necessarily microscopic, seaweed; in a marine aquarium, particularly one unwanted by the aquarist

microbiota (͵mīkrō͵bī'ōd·ȧ) — living organisms of a particular habitat that are too small to be seen with the unaided human eye

microcrustacean (͵mīkrō͵krȧ ͵stāshȧn) — any tiny to microscopic species, such as a copepod

microeinstein (͵mīkrō͵īnz͵tīn) — a unit of measure of light energy

microfauna — collectively, the tiny to microscopic animals found in a specific habitat

microinvertebrates — any tiny to microscopic animals of any phylum lacking a spinal column

micronutrients — food compounds required by an organism only in very small quantities

microplankton — free-swimming, tiny to microscopic plants and animals constituting an important source of food in both freshwater and marine habitats

microscope — a device for enlarging, by means of either optical or electronic lenses, objects too small to be observed by the naked eye

microscope

Microsorium (͵mīkrō͵sōrēȧm) — Java fern, a nonflowering freshwater plant easily propagated in aquariums

microsymbiont (͵mīkrō͵simbē͵änt) . — the smaller organism in a relationship in which two species are characteristically found in each other's presence

midwater — the area extending from a few inches below the surface to a few inches above the bottom; certain species are adapted for life in this region

milfoil — vinelike plants, *Myriophyllum* species, of freshwater habitats having finely divided foliage, often kept in aquariums; an introduced pest in some waters of the United States

Millepora (ˌmiləˈpōrə) — commonly known as fire coral, hydrozoans, found in all seas, that produce calcified skeletons superficially similar to that of scleractinians; contact with their living tissues can produce a painful, burning sensation accompanied by inflammation and swelling

milliequivalent — one thousandth of one chemical equivalent, or the amount of acid or alkalai required to exactly neutralize a 0.001 normal solution

milt — the exudate of a male fish that contains his sperm cells

mimicry — an adaptation in which one organism evolves to resemble another, thereby gaining some survival benefit

minireef — an aquarium in which a variety of marine invertebrate species, particularly corals, is exhibited in a naturalistic setting

mitochondrion (ˈmīd·əˌkändrēən) — in eukaryotic organisms, the subcellular structure in which energy obtained from food molecules is chemically stored in a form available for distribution throughout the cell

Moenkhausia (mōˈənˌk(h)äwsēə) — South American characins with silvery, sometimes translucent bodies

and often a prominent dark spot on the caudal peduncle

Mollienesia (ˌmälēəˈnēs(y)ēə) — a now-invalid, but still often-cited name for certain live-bearing fish of the Family Poecillidae found in brackish waters in North and Central America

mollusk — any member of Phylum Mollusca, invertebrates such as clams, snails, chitons, and octopus, that share specific anatomical and developmental characters

mollusk

molly — any of the species of *Poecillia*, formerly *Mollinesia*, from North and Central American brackish habitats, the most popular of which is a solid black color form

molybdenum — a chemical element (Md) required in trace amounts by certain nitrifying bacteria

Monacanthus (ˈmänəˌkan(th)thəs) — filefish, marine species of Family Monacanthidae, often with rough scales from which the common name is derived; several species are suitable for the marine aquarium, depending upon their feeding requirements

Monodactylus (ˌmä(ˌ)nōˈdaktələs) — monos, large, silvery fish of Family Monodactylidae; primarily herbivorous; they are maintained in brackish water aquariums

monoecious — said of angiosperms bearing both male and female flowers on the same plant

monospecific genus — genus containing only a single species

monotypic — a taxonomic group containing only one subordinate member, such as a monospecific genus (*see* MONOSPECIFIC GENUS)

Montipora ('mäntə‚pōrə) — a small-polyped, branching stony coral easily propagated in the aquarium by means of cuttings

Mopsella ('mäp‚sələ) — colorful gorgonian soft corals, often found in deep water, which are regularly imported and adapt well to the marine aquarium if provided with sufficient food

mormyrid ((')mȯ(r)ˈmīrəd) — elephant nose fish, Family Mormyridae; restricted to Africa, they are largely peaceful and nocturnal species capable of generating and detecting weak electrical charges by which they probably locate food and/or communicate

Mormyrus (mȯ(r)ˈmīrəs) — type genus of the elephant nose fish family

morphology — the study of anatomical structure and its development in living organisms

morph — a particular type, usually denoted by a characteristic color pattern, within a species

mouth — the anterior opening of the digestive tract, into which food is ingested

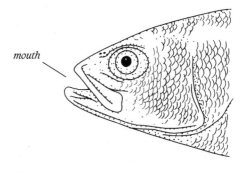

mouth

mouthbrooder — any fish, but particularly certain cichlids, in which the fertilized eggs are incubated within the oral cavity of a parent

mouthbrooder

mucosa (myüˈkōsə) — a layer of tissue that secretes mucus, usually lining a body cavity in contact with the external environment

mucus — a viscous secretion produced by specialized epidermal cells that serves to lubricate and protect tissue surfaces in contact with the external environment

mulm ('məlm) — undecomposed fish wastes and other solid matter that accumulates in the aquarium as a fine, brownish, fluffy material requiring periodic removal by siphoning

multinucleate — condition of a cell having more than one organelle bearing the genetic material

Muraena (myü'rēnə) — moray eels, Family Muraenidae, nocturnal marine fish with an elongate body and strong dentition; they prey on other fish and large invertebrates; easily maintained in a large aquarium

Murex ('myù,reks) — a genus of snails, worldwide in distribution, often predators of other mollusks; sometimes kept in marine aquariums because of their attractively ornamented shells

mutualism — a symbiotic relationship in which two species typically live together, each benefitting the other

Mylossoma ('mīlə,sōmə) — large vegetarian characins, related to piranhas, subfamily Serrasalminae, found from the southern Amazon to Argentina; easily maintained in aquariums of suitable proportions

myomere — one of the blocks of muscle tissue along each side of the body of a fish

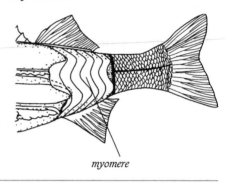

myomere

Myriophyllum (,mīrēō'fīləm) — milfoil, aquatic plants with feathery leaves that are often kept in garden ponds and aquariums

mysis shrimp ('mīsəs 'shrimp) — also called "opossum shrimp," any crustacean of the Class Mysidacea; often harvested from the sea and frozen as a food for aquarium fish

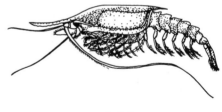

mysis shrimp

N

Nandus ('nan(͵)düs) — type genus of the Family Nandidae, predatory freshwater fish of Southeast Asia

Nannostomus (͵nanō͵stōməs) — pencilfish, South American characins that do best in soft, acid water with a lot of plants and a diet of planktonlike foods

Nanochromis (͵nanō͵krōməs) — small, beautiful cichlids of the Zaire River and its tributaries, suitable for a planted community tank

Narcine ('när͵sēn) — electric rays, marine elasmobranchs able to generate an electric shock of about 20 volts; they are exhibited in specialized aquariums

Naso (͵nāzō) — large acanthurid fish of the Indo-Pacific; the males often develop a protuberance from the center of the forehead; they are suitable only for large aquariums, but regularly imported

nauplius ('nȯplēəs) — the first instar, or larval stage, of a crustacean such as the brine shrimp, *Artemia salina*

necropsy — dissection of a dead animal specimen, usually to determine the cause of death

necrosis — death and deterioration of the tissues of a living organism as a result of disease or injury

Nemateleotris ('nemə'teleōtrəs) — fire dart gobies, Family Gobidae, popular with marine aquarium enthusiasts because of their bright coloration and propensity to hover motionless in midwater; they feed on a variety of planktonic organisms

Nematobrycon ('neməd·ə'brīkən) — emperor tetras, characins from western Columbia that do well in planted aquariums

nematocyst ('neməd·ə͵sist) — a subcellular structure consisting of a projectile, ejected upon stimulation by external contact, employed for prey capture and defense, and found only in cnidarians

nematode ('nemə'tōd) — roundworm, any member of Phylum Nematoda; certain species are important in the aquarium either as parasites of fish and invertebrates or as an organism cultivated for feeding to certain fish

nematode

Nemenzophyllia ('nē mən͵zō͵ fil(y)ēə) — a stony coral in which the individual polyps are disklike, about an inch in diameter, and arrayed along the top edge of a wall-like skeletal structure; often displayed in minireef aquariums

nemertean (nǝ'mǝrd·ēǝn) — ribbon worms, Phylum Nemertea, marine and rarely terrestrial invertebrates with an elongate, flattened body and a proboscis retractible into a sheath on the anterior end; colorful species are sometimes introduced into the aquarium living within a rock cavity

Neocirrhites (ˌnē(ˌ)ō'sǝrēd·ēs) — one of several genera of hawkfish, Family Cirrhitidae, including the popular flame hawkfish, *N. armatus*

Neolamprologus (ˌnē(ˌ)ō'lamprǝ 'lōgǝs) — one of many cichlid genera of the African rift lakes

Neolebias (ˌnē(ˌ)ō'lǝ'bēǝs) — small African characins with distinctive color differences between the sexes; suitable for soft, acid water in planted aquariums

night coloring — a pattern, often strikingly different from the one assumed during daylight, adopted by some fish after sunset or during sleep

nitrate — (NO_3-) the end product of the metabolism of ammonia by nitrifying bacteria; it must be periodically removed from aquarium water to prevent harm to the inhabitants

nitrification — the oxidation of ammonia to nitrate by means of cer-

tain bacteria; the process of biological filtration as it occurs in the aquarium

$$I. \ 2NH_3 + 3O_2 \longrightarrow 2NO_2^- + 2H^+ + 2H_2O$$

$$II. \ 2NO_2^- + O_2 \longrightarrow 2NO_3^-$$

nitrification

nitrifier — any of the bacteria capable of ammonia oxidation

nitrifying bacteria — those prokaryotic organisms that collectively carry out nitrification, or biological filtration

nitrite — (NO_2^-) a toxic anion intermediate formed in the process of ammonia oxidation carried out in the aquarium by certain bacteria

Nitrobacter (ˌnī·(ˌ)trō,baktǝ(r)) — a genus of bacteria once thought to be solely responsible for oxidation of nitrite to nitrate during biological filtration; recent research has shown that other genera are more likely involved

nitrofurazone (ˌnī·(ˌ)trō'fyu̇rǝ,zōn) — one of several antibiotics effective in the treatment of diseases of marine aquarium fish, although several pathogens are resistant

nitrogen — the chemical element (N_2), a gas comprising most of the atmosphere and present in thousands of biologically important compounds

nitrogen cycle — the natural process through which nitrogen incorporated into food molecules by photosynthetic organisms is consumed directly or indirectly by other organisms and subsequently excreted, acted upon by bacteria, and made available again for plant nutrition

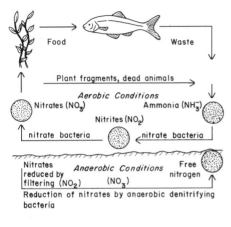

nitrogen cycle

Nitrosomonas (ˌnī·(ˌ)trō'sämənəs) — a genus of bacteria once thought to be solely responsible for oxidation of ammonia to nitrite during biological filtration; recent research has shown that other genera are more likely involved

nocturnal — active primarily during the hours of darkness

nonphotosynthetic (ˌnänˌfōd·ō'sinˌthed·ik) — unable to produce food from simple molecules, thus relying on food produced by organisms with this ability

nostril — in fish, an external opening leading to the pharynx

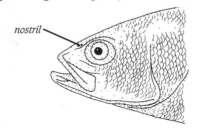

Nothobranchius (ˌnäthəˌbraŋkēəs) — African killifish known as "annuals" because they hatch, mature, and reproduce within a single season; they are popular with specialized freshwater hobbyists

Notopterus (nō'täptərəs) — the clown knifefish, *N. chitala*, a nocturnal, predatory Asian species that can be maintained in large aquariums if fed live foods exclusively

Novaculichthyes (nō'vaˌkyülikˌth(y)ēəs) — dragon wrasses, Family Labridae, imported for the marine aquarium as juveniles with striking green, white, and black coloration; adults reach about a foot (30 cm) in length

nudibranch ('n(y)üdəˌbraŋk) — any member of the molluscan Order Nudibranchia, marine snails lacking a shell and with the gills exposed and often retractable; often attempted by aquarium hobbyists because of their brilliant coloration, they are difficult to maintain successfully due to their specialized dietary requirements

Nuphar ('n(y)üfə(r)) — spatter-docks, members of the water lily family found along the Atlantic coast of North America and sometimes grown in large aquariums and ponds; their flowers are not as showy as the true water lilies

nutrient — any molecule that serves as food for a living organism

Nymphaea (nim'fēə) — true water lilies, native to North America and

Asia, dwarf varieties of which are sometimes kept in freshwater aquariums; all types are frequently cultivated in garden ponds

Nymphoides (nim'fó(y)dēz) — banana plants, small members of the water lily family in which the roots of adventitious plantlets resemble a bunch of bananas, often grown as a novelty in freshwater aquariums

occiput ('äksə(,)pət) — the area where the dorsal musculature attaches to the skull of a fish

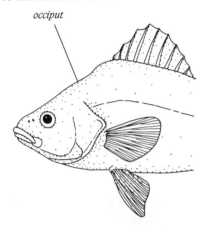

occiput

octocoral — any member of the anthozoan Subclass Octocorallia, including soft corals and gorgonians, in which the tentacles are arranged in multiples of eight

octopod — any species of octopus or argonaut, cephalopod mollusks with eight arms surrounding the mouth

Octopus ('äktəpəs) — octopus, cephalopods with eight tentacles bearing suckers for attachment and prey capture

Oculina (,äkyə'līnə) — eye coral, a branching stony coral with prominent corallites, found in the Atlantic and Gulf of Mexico and sometimes colonizing live rock produced in these areas

Odontosyllus (ō,dän·'tō'siləs) — stomatopod crustaceans commonly known as "mantis shrimp" because their raptorial appendages resemble those of the praying mantis insect

olfactory — of or having to do with the sense of smell

oligochaete ('äləgō,kēt) — segmented worms of the annelid Class Oligochaeta, nonparasitic forms with few bristles on the segments, such as the common earthworm; certain aquatic species are cultivated as fish food

omnivore ('ämnə,vō(ə)r) — an organism that feeds on both plant and animal matter

oocyte ('ōə,sīt) — the cell that gives rise to the egg

Oodinium (,ōe'dinēəm) — a microscopic dinoflagellate parasite of freshwater fish, producing the condition known as "velvet disease"; usually fatal if not treated

Oodinium

opaque — impervious to light

opercle (ō'pərkəl) — the flap that covers the gills of fish

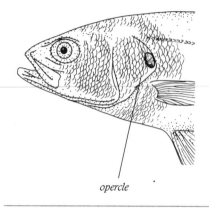

opercle

operculum (ō'pərkyələm) — in snails and some annelids, a calcified or proteinaceous plate used to cover the opening of the shell when the animal is withdrawn inside

Ophioblennius (ˌäfē(ˌ)ō'blenēəs) — an Atlantic genus in the Family Blennidae, the most commonly imported species of which is *O. atlanticus*, the red-lipped blenny

Ophioderma (ˌäfē(ˌ)ō'dərmə) — a common genus of serpent stars collected in the Atlantic

ophiuroid (ˌäfē'(y)ùrȯ(y)d) — any member of the echinoderm Class Ophiuroidea, the serpent and brittle stars, characterized by a disk-shaped body from which radiate five flexible arms bearing tube feet; in some members the arms branch repeatedly, giving the impression of many more than five

opisthobranch (ə'pisthəˌbraŋk) — snails of Subclass Opisthobranchia, that have a single gill and share similarities of larval development, and among which loss or reduction of the shell and bilateral symmetry are common traits

Opisthognathus (ˌäpəs'thägnəˌthəs) — type genus of the jawfish, Family Opisthognathidae, the only common aquarium species of which is the yellow-headed jawfish, *O. aurifrons*

oral disc — the upper surface of an anemone, bearing the tentacles and with the mouth in the center

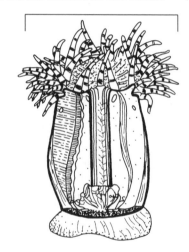

oral disc

orbit length — the maximum diameter of the eye of a fish

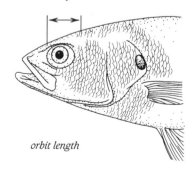

orbit length

Oreaster (ōr͵ēstə(r)) — sea stars typified by the large West Indian species *O. reticulata*, which is predatory on sessile invertebrates

Orectolobus (ō͵rek'täləbəs) — nurse sharks, Family Orectolobidae, with distinctive nasal barbels; a usually sluggish and sedentary species that can adapt to very large aquariums

organelle (¦ȯ(r)gə¦nel) — any of various membrane-bound subcellular structures found within the cells of eukaryotic organisms

organic matter — any substance produced by a living organism; usually refers to nonliving remains, excreta, or the like

ORP — oxidation-reduction potential, the tendency for oxidation reactions to occur in a solution, determined by measuring the electrical potential in millivolts across a standardized electrode; an oxidation potential above 400 mV is considered a sign of good water conditions in a marine aquarium

orthophosphate (¦ȯ(r)thə'fäs͵fāt) — phosphate, PO_4^{3-}, as measured in tests used for aquarium water

Oryzias (ō'rīzēəs) — rice fish, or medakas, the most primitive cyprinodontid fish, from Indonesia and Southeast Asia

oscar — *Astronotus ocellatus*, an Amazonian cichlid extremely popular with aquarium hobbyists because of its tendency to develop an individual "personality" and to recognize its owner

osculum ('äskyələm) — the opening through which water is discharged from the body of a sponge

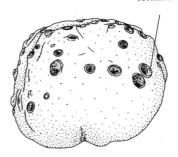

osculum

osmoregulation (¦äzmō'regyə'lāshen) — control of the water and electrolyte balance in the body of a living organism

osmosis (͵äz'mōsəs) — the movement of water molecules across a semipermeable membrane from an area of higher solute concentration to an area of lower solute concentration

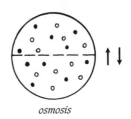

osmosis

osomotic pressure — the tendency of water to move across a semipermeable membrane, as a consequence of the difference between solute concentrations on either side

Osphronemus (ˌäsfrəˈnēməs) — the giant gourami, Asian anabantid fish sometimes exhibited in large freshwater aquariums

Osteoglossum (ˌästēōˈgläsəm) — bony-tongued fish, Family Osteoglossidae, primitive species known in the aquarium trade as "arrowanas"; the most common species is from South America

Ostracion (äˈstrās(h)ēən) — type genus of the boxfish family, Ostraciidae, marine fish in which the body is enclosed in a shell made of interlocking bony plates instead of scales

outgassing — the escape of free gasses, such as carbon dioxide or oxygen, from the surface of a container or body of water

ovaries — organs in which eggs are produced

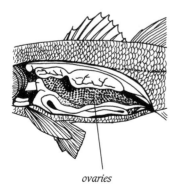

ovaries

oviparous ((ˈ)ōˌvipərəs) — reproduction by means of eggs released into the environment

oviparous

ovipositor (ˈōvəˌpäzəd·ə(r)) — a structure through which a female fish or invertebrate introduces eggs on or into a suitable substrate for incubation

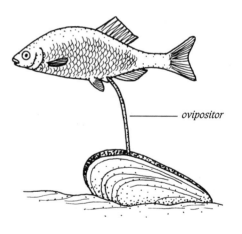

ovipositor

ovoviviparous (ˌō(ˌ)vōˈvīˌvip(ə)rəs) — mode of reproduction in which fertilized eggs are incubated within the body of one parent, usually the female, and the young are released as fully formed miniatures of the adults

ovoviviparous

Oxycirrhites (ˌäksē'sȧrēd·əs) — hawkfish, Family Cirrhitidae, the most popular member of which is the longnosed hawkfish, *O. typus*, from the Indo-Pacific

oxygen — a chemical element existing normally as the colorless, odorless gaseous form, O_2, and required by all living organisms, with the exception of certain bacteria, for the metabolism of food

Oxymonacanthus (ˌäksē'mänəˌkan(t)thəs) — the only commonly imported species of this genus, *O. longirostris*, the orange-spotted filefish; it seldom adapts to the aquarium because it normally feeds only on coral polyps

ozone — the triatomic form of oxygen, O_3, with a characteristic odor; it is used in aquarium husbandry as a disinfectant and to increase the ORP value of the water

ozonization — the process of introducing triatomic oxygen directly into aquarium water

ozonizer — a device for the production of ozone, usually by exposing air to an electric spark

P

paddlefish — two primitive freshwater fish, *Polyodon* and *Pseuphurus*, that feed by swimming open-mouthed to trap planktonic organisms; sometimes exhibited in large aquariums as a curiosity

Padina (pə'dīnə) — a brown seaweed shaped like a small fan attached at the pointed end to a solid substrate

Paguristes (pə'gyù,rēstəs) — the scarlet hermit crab, *P. cadenanti*, often imported from the tropical Atlantic for algae control in the marine aquarium

Pagurus (pəgyùrəs) — hermit crabs, typified by the small species, *P. longicarpus*, from the temperate Atlantic; it is often added to marine aquariums as a scavenger

Palaemonetes (pə'lē,män,ētēs) — glass or rock shrimps, often sold for fresh or brackish water aquariums or as fish food

pallial line — a scar marking the area of mantle attachment on the inside of the shell of a bivalve mollusk; useful in identification

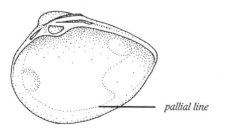

pallial line

Palythoa ('pālē'thōə) — zoanthids, colonial anthozoans of which several species are collected for the aquarium, consisting of several short polyps connected at the base by a sheet of tissue

Panchax ('pan,chəks) — an outdated name for numerous species of cyprinodontoid fish now mostly assigned to *Aphyosemion* and *Epiplatys*; the name persists in both aquarium literature and the trade

Pangasius (pän,gäsēəs) — large, predatory Asian catfish species, the most popular of which, *P. sutchii*, is known in the aquarium trade as the "iridescent shark"

Pantodon ('pantə,dän) — the African butterflyfish, *P. bucholzi*, the only member of this genus of surface-dwelling, insect-eating fish regularly seen in the aquarium trade

Paracheirodon (parə'kī,rōdon) — the neon tetra, *P. innesi*, native to the middle and upper Amazon River of South America, among the most popular species for the freshwater community aquarium; it is closely related to the cardinal tetra, *P. axelrodi*

parapod — one of the leglike appendages of polychaete annelid worms

parapod

parasite — an organism living on or within another organism; it provides no benefit to its host, but often harms it

parasiticide — any substance used to kill parasites

parasitism — the symbiotic relationship between a parasite and its host

parrotfish — any of the marine Family Scaridae, in which the teeth are fused into a beak strong enough to allow them to bite off chunks of living stony corals, from which they digest the polyps and excrete the skeletal material as sand; seldom adaptable to the home aquarium

parthenogenesis (¦pärthənō'jenəsəs) — the development of a new individual from an unfertilized egg

particle filter — any device designed for removal of tiny flecks of unwanted matter from aquarium water (*see* MECHANICAL FILTRATION)

pathogenic — disease producing, as of bacteria

Pavona (pə'vōnə) — lettuce corals, delicate stony corals in which the polyps protrude from a thin, leaflike skeleton; they will reproduce themselves in the marine aquarium

pearlfish — any of several species of *Carapus*, such as *C. bermudensis*, that live in the digestive tract of certain star fish and sea cucumbers, such as *Actinopyga agassizi*; they emerge at night to feed on small organisms and return to the cucumber by day, causing it no apparent harm

pectoral fin — the most anterior of the paired appendages of a fish, homologous to the arms of higher vertebrates

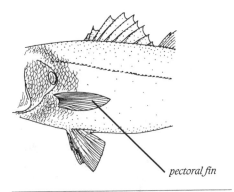

pectoral fin

pedal disc — the flattened base of the column of a sea anemone or other solitary polyp; the animal uses it to attach itself to a solid surface

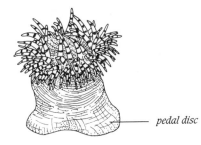

pedal disc

pedicillaria (ˌpedəˌsila(a)rēə) — specialized appendages numerous on the body surface of many echinoderms; they are pincerlike, often venomous, and used both in defense and in the removal of foreign matter

peduncle — the fleshy lobe by which a fin is attached

pelagic — living primarily in open water, rather than in association with a solid surface

pelecypod (pəlɘsəˌpäd) — any bivalve mollusk, such as an oyster or clam

pelecypod

pelvic fin — the most posterior paired appendages of a fish, homologous to the legs of other vertebrates, located on the ventral surface anterior to the anus

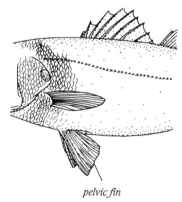

pelvic fin

Pelvicachromis ('pelvē'kəˌkrōməs) — *P. pulcher*, the kribensis cichlid, and other freshwater species from central Africa that are suitable for a community aquarium, typically reaching about 4 inches (10 cm) in length

Penicillus (ˌpenə'siləs) — green seaweed known as "merman's shaving brush," arising from the substrate as a short stalk topped with a thick, round tuft of filaments

Pentacta ('pen·ˌtaktə) — *P. pygmaea*, the red-footed sea cucumber, imported for the aquarium from the Gulf of Mexico; it feeds on microorganisms strained from the water

Periclimenes (perəˌklīmənəs) — one of several shrimps that live in association with sea anemones in tropical environments worldwide; they are often imported and make good aquarium subjects

Periophthalmus (ˌperēˌäf'thalməs) — mudskippers, semiterrestrial fish of the mangrove swamps and estuaries of the West African coast, Southeast Asia, and Australia; often exhibited in brackish-water aquariums

Petrochirus (ˌpe·trō'kīrəs) — hermit crabs from the tropical Atlantic, often collected as small specimens, but becoming large and too aggressive for most aquariums

Petrolisthes ('pe·trəˌlīs(t)thəs) — porcelain crabs, including several colorful species that live in association with sea anemones in the Indo-Pacific; frequently seen in the aquarium trade

pH — the negative logarithm of the hydrogen ion concentration of a solution; pure water is at 7.0 on this scale, with acidity of the solution increasing below this point and alkalinity likewise increasing above this point; aquarium waters are usually in the range of 6.0 to 8.5, depending upon the environment being replicated (*see* APPENDIX 1: MEASUREMENTS, EQUIVALENTS, AND FORMULAS)

phagocytosis (ˌfagəˌsīˈtōsəs) — intake of solid food by a living cell through a process of engulfment

pharyngeal teeth (fəˈriŋgəl ˈtēth) — those located on the modified gill arches of certain fish, notably the carp family, Cyprinidae

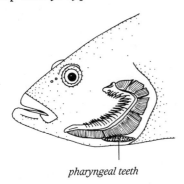

pharyngeal teeth

phenolphthalein (ˈfēnōl(f)ˈthalēən) — a chemical indicator sometimes used for simple determinations of pH

phenotypic (ˈfēnə·tipik) — the actual expression in an individual of the genetic traits inherited from its parents; the observable characteristics of an organism resulting from the interaction of its environment and its genes

phoresis (feˈrēsəs) — literally, "carrying," used to describe the habit in some organisms of attaching objects to themselves for camouflage

phoresis

phoronid (ˈfəˈrōnəd) — a tube-dwelling worm that feeds by means of a specialized spiral structure, the lophophore, sometimes found on live rock imported for the marine aquarium

phosphorescent (ˌfäsfəˈresᵊnt) — in physics, said of a substance that continues to emit light for a time after the source of energizing radiation is removed; in popular aquarium literature, often said of any organism that produces light

phosphorus — a chemical element (P) important in energy transformation reactions in living cells, and essential to all organisms

photobiologist — one who studies photobiology

photobiology — the science of the interactions between living organisms and light

Photoblepharon ('fōd·(,)ō'blefərən) — the flashlight fish, a deep-water marine species sometimes exhibited in aquariums, possessing a light organ underneath each eye that contains symbiotic, bioluminescent bacteria

photoperiod — the relative exposure of an organism to daylight as a proportion of the total 24-hour day

photoperiodicity — exhibiting a cycle of behavior coordinated with the day-night cycle

photopigment — a colored chemical compound, such as chlorophyll, that absorbs energy from light

photosynthesis — the process by which plants, some bacteria, and certain protists use light energy to manufacture food molecules, thus forming the basis for most of Earth's food webs

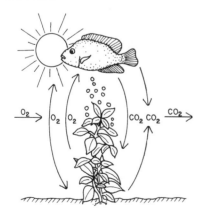

photosynthesis

photosynthesizer — any organism capable of photosynthesis

phototaxis — specific movement toward or away from light; in the former case the movement is said to be positive, in the latter case, negative

phototaxis

Phoxinus ('fō'kīnəs) — North American cyprinids commonly known as "dace"; they are kept in temperate freshwater aquariums because of the bright coloration of the breeding males

phyletic (fī'led·ik) — referring to the evolutionary history of a taxon

phylogenetic (¦fīlō'jə'ned·ik) — having to do with the evolutionary history of groups of organisms

Phymanthus (fī'man(t)thəs) — shallow-water sea anemones from tropical Florida and the West Indies, known as "flower anemones" in the aquarium trade

Physogyra (¦fīsə'jīrə) — stony corals with bubblelike tentacles on the polyps; easily maintained in minireef aquariums

phytophagus (fītä'fāgəs) — feeding primarily on plant matter

phytophagus

phytoplankton (¦fīd·ə'plaŋktən) — photosynthetic organisms swimming or suspended in the water column, and important as the basis for aquatic food webs

picric acid — a toxic chemical sometimes used in low concentrations as a parasiticidal dip for freshwater or marine aquarium fish

pigmentation — having color, or the color pattern of an organism such as a fish

Pimelodus (¸pimə¸lōdəs) — South American catfish, Family Pimelodidae, of rapid movement, bearing long barbels; they are predatory

pinnate — feather-like

pinnules — the smallest subdivisions of the arms or branches of

certain invertebrates, or a subdivision of a leaf that is twice or more divided

pinocytosis (¦pinō'sīd·ō¸səs) — intake of liquid by a living cell through a process of engulfment

pipefish — any member of the Family Syngnathidae with an elongate body not holding the head at right angles to the spine; closely related to seahorses

piscatorial — having to do with an interest in fish

Pistia ('pistēə) — water lettuce, a floating neotropical flowering plant of the *Arum* family often exhibited in garden ponds and large freshwater aquariums

placoid scale — thick, enamel-like epidermal structures found in elasmobranch fish; their toothlike ornamentation gives the animal a rough, sandpaperlike surface texture

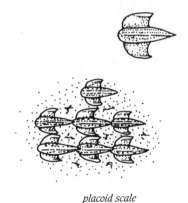

placoid scale

Plagiotremus (¸plājē'ä·trēməs) — scale- or flesh-nipping blennies that mimic harmless species in order to get within striking range of their prey; sometimes exhibited as aquarium curiosities

plankter — any organism comprising the plankton

planktivore (('plaŋkˌtiv(ə)r) — any organism feeding primarily on plankton

planktivore

plankton — unicellular and small multicellular organisms, both plant and animal, suspended or swimming in the water column, forming an important food source for numerous other organisms

plankton

planula ('planyələ) — the two-layered, ciliated, free-swimming larval stage of many cnidarians, including stony corals

planula

Platax ('plātəks) — batfish, Family Platacidae, tropical marine fish of which only one species (*P. obicularis*) is commonly successful in an aquarium

Plecostomus (plə'kōstəməs) — South American loricariid catfish with a mouth adapted for rasping food from logs and stones; the name is often applied to any similar fish by aquarium dealers

Plectorhynchus (plək'tō'riŋkəs) — sweetlips, tropical marine fish, Family Gasterinidae, with bold brown and white coloration and unusual swimming movements; they unfortunately seldom adapt to a diet of aquarium foods

pleopod — a swimming leg located on the abdomen of a crustacean

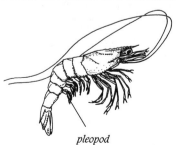

pleopod

Plerogyra (plə'rō'jīrə) — bubble corals, stony corals popular with minireef hobbyists because of their unusual bulbous tentacles

Plexaura ('pleksə(r)ə) — gorgonian soft corals often imported for minireef aquariums

Plotosus (plə'tōsəs) — marine catfish, the juveniles of which are attractively striped in yellow and black and exhibit schooling behavior; they grow to become large, aggressive, gray-colored adults

Pocillopora (pō'silō'pərə) — a large genus of small-polyped stony corals that can be readily propagated from cuttings

Podochela ('pädə,kələ) — a spider crab found in the Gulf of Mexico and collected for the aquarium because it characteristically covers its carapace with living invertebrates and algae collected from its immediate surroundings

Poecilia (,pō'sil(y)ēə) — type genus of Family Poecillidae, the livebearers, including such perennial aquarium favorites as the guppy *P. reticulata*, and mollies *P. latipinna* and *P. velifera*

poikilothermic (po(y)'kilə,thərmik) — referring to organisms lacking the ability to regulate body temperature, and thus assuming the ambient temperature; cold-blooded

polychaete ('pälē'kēt) — segmented marine worms in the annelid Class Polychaeta bearing numerous bristles on the segments; there are some 15,000 species

polyp ('päləp) — the flowerlike form in the life cycle of most cnidarians; it consists of a column attached at the base to a substrate or, in colonial forms, to another portion of the colony, and is topped with an oral disc consisting of the tissues surrounding the mouth and forming an encircling ring of tentacles

Polypterus (pəlip,tərəs) — bichirs, primitive, predatory lobe-finned fish of central Africa that are popular for specialized aquariums

polytrophic — having more than one mode of nutrition

Pomacanthus (¦pōmə'kan(t)thəs) — large marine angelfish in the Family Pomacanthidae, in which the juveniles are colored much differently from the adults; beautiful but demanding aquarium subjects

popeye — a synonym for the pathological condition exopthalmus

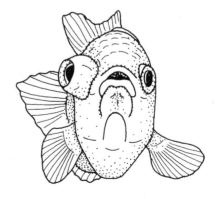

popeye

poriferan (pərif(ə)rən) — a sponge, any animal of Phylum Porifera

Porites (pərīd·(,)ēz) — type genus of the large stony coral Family Poritidae; many species are known and most are rather challenging to maintain in a marine reef aquarium

post-orbit length — the distance from the posterior edge of the eye to the anterior edge of the opercle

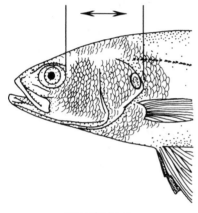

post-orbit length

Potamogeton (,päd·əmō'jētän) — pondweeds, aquatic flowering plants of both tropical and temperate lacustrine and fluvial habitats

potassium — a chemical element (K) required by all living organisms

power filter — any water purification device that operates by pumping water under pressure through a medium

powerhead — a small submersible water pump, so named because the first models were intended for installation at the top, or "head," of the airlift on an undergravel filter, replacing the air supply system and supposedly increasing filtration "power"

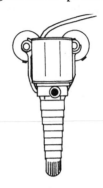

powerhead

ppb — parts per billion, equivalent to micrograms per liter

ppm — parts per million, equivalent to milligrams per liter

ppt — parts per thousand, equivalent to grams per liter

predatory — descriptive of any animal that actively seeks out other living animals and consumes them

predatory

prefilter — any contrivance intended to protect filtration equipment from damage by preventing the intake of oversized objects, or to protect aquarium specimens from entrapment by filtration equipment, or both

Premnas (prem'nəs) — spine-cheeked anemonefish, including the single species, *P. biaculeatus* and its color varieties; all are popular with marine aquarium enthusiasts

preoperculum ('prē'ō'pərkyələm) — the area just anterior to the gill cover of many fish

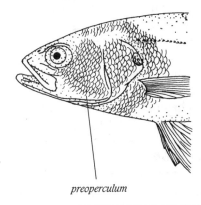

preoperculum

Pristella (pristələ) — X-ray fish or pristella, characins from the Amazon Basin, now produced in captivity for the aquarium trade; long popular among hobbyists as community fish

prokaryote (prō'kareōt) — a living organism lacking a membrane-bound nucleus containing the genetic material, or any other subcellular components surrounded by a membrane and including Kingdom Monera, the bacteria

propagation — increase in the numbers of a species by human intervention

protandrous hermaphroditism (prōd·andrəs hə(r)'mafrə'dīd·ˌizəm) — a condition of some species in which individuals begin life as males and later change to females as a result of maturation or environmental stimuli

protein — a polymer of amino acids specified by one gene; the millions of kinds of such molecules perform a variety of essential functions in all living cells

protein skimmer — any water purification device that removes dissolved organic and inorganic matter from water by their sequestration on the surfaces of air bubbles, and is so designed as to trap the viscous, greenish brown foam that is produced in a receptacle from which it can be periodically discarded

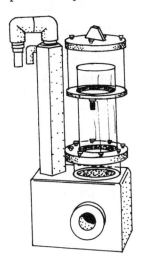

protein skimmer

protein skimming — the utilization of a protein skimmer for aquarium water purification

proteinaceous ('prō͵te͵nāshəs) — composed of protein

protist — a unicellular organism

protogynous hermaphroditism (͵prōd·ə͵jīnəs hə(r)'mafrə'dīd·͵izəm) — a condition of some species in which individuals begin life as females and later change to males as a result of maturation or environmental stimuli

protozoan — an animal-like protist; also sometimes refers to any protist

Pseudanthias (͵südə'anthēəs) — small sea basses, Family Serranidae, that form shoals dominated by a single, distinctively colored male, and feed upon plankton in shallow water; numerous species are imported for marine aquariums

Pseudochromis ͵südō'krōməs) — dottybacks, small sea basses, Family Serranidae, of the Indo-Pacific region that can be propagated in commercial quantities for the aquarium trade; there are several species

Pseudocolochirus ('südō'kōlō'kirəs) — sea apples, brightly colored holothurids from the Indo-Pacific, often imported for the marine reef aquarium despite their poisonous flesh and eggs

Pseudopterogorgia ('südō'terō ͵gorjēə) — sea feathers, gorgonian soft corals with the branches arranged in a single plane, superficially resembling a bird's feather

Pseudotropheus (͵sü͵dō'trōfēəs) — a cichlid of the African rift lakes, many species of which are popular with aquarium hobbyists

Ptereleotris (tərə͵lēōd·ris) — torpedo gobies, Family Gobidae, sometimes imported for marine aquariums, although inclined to jump from the tank if disturbed

Pterogorgia ('terō͵gorjēə) — sea feathers, gorgonian soft corals with the branches arranged in a single plane, superficially resembling a bird's feather

Pterois ('terəwəs) — lionfish, any of several species in Family Scorpaenidae that reach an adult length greater than 6 inches (15 cm); all have venomous dorsal and pectoral fin spines

Pterolebias (͵terə'lǝbēəs) — South American fish, Family Rivulidae, that bury their eggs to protect them from seasonal drought

Pterophyllum (͵tərə'fīləm) — South American freshwater angelfish, Family Cichlidae, including *P. scalare* and its numerous varieties and forms; popular with hobbyists for decades

Pterosynchiropus ('tərə'siŋkərōpəs) — the mandarinfish, *P. splendidus*, Family Callyonimidae; frequently imported for the aquarium from Indo-Pacific reefs; requires tiny living foods in order to survive

puffer — any fish of the Family Tetraodontidae, able to inflate itself by drawing water into a specialized chamber, thus deterring many predators

pulmonate — having lungs for breathing atmospheric oxygen

Puntius ('pün(,)shəs) — a now-invalid name for numerous aquarium barbs, Family Cyprinidae, including the tiger barb, correctly called *Barbus tetrazona*; the name persists in the literature and among aquarium dealers

pupfish — any of several species of *Cyprinodon*, Family Cyprinodontidae, of the American Southwest and Mexico, notable for the status of many as endangered species and as inhabitants of thermal springs

Pygoplites (,pīgō'plītəs) — the regal angelfish, *P. diacanthus*, often imported for the aquarium, but seldom adaptable to captive conditions

Pylopagurus (,pīlō,pəgyürəs) — marine hermit crabs, including the trapdoor hermit, *P. operculatus*, from the tropical Atlantic; a colorful species with an enlarged, white chela that it uses to close the opening of the snail shell in which it lives

Pyramidella (pir(y)ə'midelə) — parasitic gastropods that sometimes infest giant clams and sea stars exhibited in aquariums; usually controlled by introducing a predator, such as the wrasse *Pseudocheilinus hexataenia*

Pyrrhulina (¦pir(y)ə'hülēnə) — attractive characins of the Amazon Basin, Family Lebiansinidae; they are good community fish

Q-R

quarantine tank — an aquarium intended for the temporary housing of any living specimen to assess its state of health before exhibition in a display tank in order to prevent transmission of disease to specimens already there

quinaldine (kwinəl,dēn) — a chemical anesthetic sometimes used to stun fish for veterinary extermination, or to make them easier to collect; there is some controversy about whether this is harmful to the fish or to other organisms in the area of capture

rabbitfish — any member of Family Siganidae, so named because of their herbivorous feeding habits

radiole (,rādēōl) — in certain polychaete annelids, a structure employed both for gas exchange and in food capture, and that in aquarium species is often strikingly colored

radiole

radula — the rasplike feeding appendage of certain mollusks, the structure of which is often used to distinguish among taxa

raptorial appendage — any extension of the body employed primarily for prey capture, but especially that of certain crustaceans

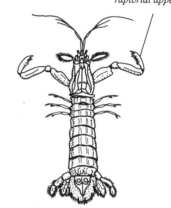

raptorial appendage

Rasbora (raz'bōrə) — small, colorful cyprinid fish native to Asia, the most common of which is the harlequin fish, *R. heteromorpha*

rasbora — common name for any fish of the genus *Rasbora*, or its close relatives

Recluzia (rə̇'klüzēə) — an unusual marine snail that feeds on pelagic hydrozoans; sometimes exhibited in specialized aquariums

redox potential — the tendency for oxidation-reduction reactions to occur, usually measured in millivolts; the higher the value, the more reactive the solution

reefkeeping — the hobby of maintaining coral reef organisms in aquariums

reflux — to pass a liquid repeatedly over an absorptive or reactive medium in order to alter the properties of the former

refugia (rə'fyüjēə) — areas deliberately provided in the design of an aquarium in which certain species can seek shelter from potential predators in the same tank

rehydrate — to add water back to anything from which it has been removed

respiration — the oxidative release of chemical energy from food molecules in a living organism

$$(CH_2O)_n + O_2 \longrightarrow CO_2 + H_2O$$

respiration

reverse osmosis (RO) unit — a water purification device that forces feed water under pressure through a semipermeable membrane, allowing only pure water with reduced solute content to pass out as the product

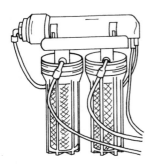

reverse osmosis (RO) unit

Rhinomuraena (,rīnō'myürēnə) — ribbon eels, Indo-Pacific fish once regularly imported for the aquarium, but seldom successfully adapted to captive conditions

Rhipocephalus (,rīpō'sēfələs) — a green seaweed with a calcified structure resembling a pinecone emerging on a stick from a solid substrate

rhizome — a rootstock, or food storage organ, formed from the root of a vascular plant, usually creeping horizontally in the substrate, and giving rise to new top growth along its length

Rhodactis ('rōdəktəs) — several species of Indo-Pacific disc anemones imported for minireef aquariums, including a bright blue form from Tonga, bearing highly branched tentacles on the oral disc

Rhynchocinetes (,riŋ(,)kō,sīnētēs) — camel shrimp, or dancing shrimp, Indo-Pacific crustaceans having a distinct hump in the carapace and found in groups often maintaining contact and coordinated movement with each other

Riccia ('richēə) — crystalwort, a floating aquatic liverwort plant of wide distribution

Ricordea (rīkord·ēə) — a false coral genus once regularly collected in Florida and the Caribbean but now largely protected by environmental regulation; it can be propagated, although slowly

Rivulus ('riv(y)ələs) — type genus of Family Rivulidae, from South America and Cuba; one species is known only from specimens in the aquarium trade

---

roe — fish eggs

---

rostrum — an extension of the anterior dorsal surface of the carapace of some crustaceans, useful in identification

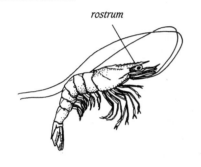

rostrum

Rotala (rō'tələ) — flowering aquatic plants in the loosestrife family with upright stems and opposite leaves, including both red and green species frequently maintained in aquariums

---

rotifer — any member of Phylum Rotifera, tiny to microscopic animals of both freshwater and marine habitats, important as a food source for many aquatic organisms; at least one species, *Brachionus plicatilus*, is employed extensively as a first food for larval marine fish

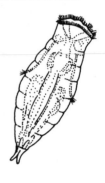

rotifer

RTN — rapid tissue necrosis, a pathological condition of stony corals caused by bacterial infection and susceptible to treatment with chloramphenicol

---

run in — to operate a new aquarium without fish for a period of time to permit the growth of desirable microorganisms and to assess equipment performance

Sabella (səbələ) — polychaetes, several species of which have colorful radioles and are often exhibited in marine aquariums

Sabellastarte (səbələ'startē) — feather duster worms, including several species from both the Atlantic and the Indo-Pacific, characterized by unusually large radioles that are rapidly withdrawn into a protective tube when the animal is disturbed

sabellid (səbəlid) — any polychaete annelid of Family Sabellidae, commonly known as fanworms or feather duster worms

Sagittaria (,sajə'ta(a)rēə) — arrowhead plant, aquatic to marsh plants of the temperate, subtropical, and tropical regions of the Americas; widely used in both aquariums and garden ponds

saline — water with sodium chloride dissolved in it, often of a precise concentration chosen to match that of the body fluids of a living organism; as an adjective, having to do with water of any salt content

salinity — a measurement of the total amount of dissolved salts in a sample of seawater, defined as the ratio of the conductivity of the seawater sample to the conductivity of a solution of 32.4356 grams (1.15 ounces) of potassium chloride per kilogram of pure water at 15°C (59°F) and 1 atmosphere; a salinity of 35 parts per thousand is considered "full-strength" seawater

Salmo ('sal(,)mō) — type genus of the Family Salmonidae, including trout and salmon, some smaller species of which are exhibited in aquariums

Salvinia ('salvēn(y)ēə) — a floating freshwater fern with pendant, fibrous roots and small, paired, rounded leaves covered with water-repellent hairs

sand — any aggregate material having grains smaller that $1/16$ inch (1.6 mm) in diameter, but large enough to be individually discernible with the unaided eye

sand dollar — the calcified test of any of several species of flattened sea urchins found on sandy sea bottoms

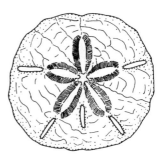

sand dollar

Sarcophyton (sär'kä,fītən) — mushroom corals, several species of alcyonarians so named because of the resemblance of the colony to the edible fungus; they are widely maintained in minireef aquariums and can be easily propagated by cuttings

Sargassum (sär'gasəm) — a brown seaweed bearing rounded, gas-filled floats often forming large masses on the ocean surface, especially the tropical Atlantic, in, under and upon which live a variety of organisms specialized for this habitat, including some that are collected for the aquarium

Saururus (sȯr(y)ürəs) — lizard's tail, a bog plant of warm temperate, subtropical, and tropical habitats in the Americas, so named because of the appearance of its flower

scale — an outgrowth of the skin of most fish, flattened and arranged in overlapping rows and variously modified depending upon species

Scarisoma (skärisōmə) — parrotfish, Family Scaridae; sometimes exhibited in large aquariums

Scarus ('ska(a)rəs) — type genus of the parrotfish family, Scaridae

Scatophagus (skatä,fāgəs) — scats, Family Scatophagidae, with round, flattened bodies, found in estuaries in Southeast Asia, East Africa, and Australia; *S. argus* is frequently imported

Schilbe ('shilbē) — Asian catfish, Family Schilbeidae, lively, schooling species sold as "mystic sharks"

schooling — fish behavior in which numerous individuals swim coordinately

schooling

scleractinian ('skler,aktin(y)ēən) — a stony coral, or member of the cnidarian Order Scleractinia

scorpionfish — any member of Family Scorpaenidae, venomous marine fish of uncertain taxonomic affiliation, but especially the species in the genus *Scorpaena*

scyphomedusa ('sī(,)fō,mə'd(y)üsə) — the body of a scyphozoan, or sea jelly

scyphozoan (sī(,)fō'zōən) — a sea jelly, any of the cnidarian Class Schyphozoa, in which the medusa is the dominant or only form that occurs during the life cycle

sea cucumber — any of the echinoderm Class Holothuroidea, so named because of the resemblance in shape of many species to the common vegetable

sea cucumber

sea grass — any marine flowering plant with straplike leaves, including species of *Thalassia* and *Syringodium*

sea grass

sea jelly — a scyphozoan, or jellyfish

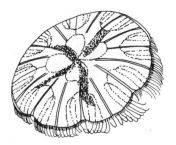

sea jelly

sea star — a starfish, or any of the echinoderm Class Asteroidea

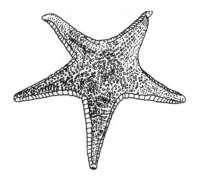

sea star

sea urchin — an echinoid, or any of the echinoderm Class Echinoidea

sea urchin

seasonality — life cycle variations coordinated with environmental changes that regularly occur at specific times of year

seawall — a structure intended to prevent erosion due to wave action

seawater — the contents of the ocean, containing, on average, 35 grams (1.24 ounces) of dissolved solids per liter

seaweed — any marine alga visible to the unaided eye, especially one having a structure superficially similar to a terrestrial plant

seaweed

sedentary — spending most or all of one's time in the same spot

segment — a repeated body element

segment

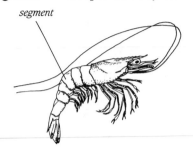

septa — walls that separate a biological structure, especially those in the corallites of stony corals

septicemia (ˌseptəˈsēmēə) — a pathological condition in which bacteria grow in the blood

Seriatopora ('sir(y)ē,tōpərə) — a branching, small-polyped stony coral easily propagated from cuttings

serpulid ('sərpyələd) — a polychaete in which the radioles are arranged in one or more spiral structures, and that secretes a protective, calcified tube around itself

Serranocirrhitus (sərənō,sərid·əs) — a solitary sea bass, Family Serranidae, from deep waters in the Indo-Pacific; often exhibited in reef aquariums and adapts readily to captivity

Serrasalmus (¦serə¦sal(,)məs) — one genus of piranhas, South American predatory characins with an undeserved reputation for human fatalities; they are often chosen for single-species aquariums

sessile (ses,īl) — among animals, one that is attached to a substrate

shell — a calcareous integument enclosing the body of an animal, but especially that of a mollusk

shell

shock — a physiological response to stress or injury; also, a flow of electricity through the body of an organism

shoreward — in the direction away from the open sea

shrimp — any small crustacean, but especially a decapod of Order Natantia

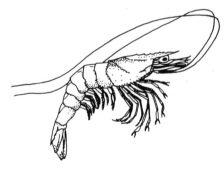

shrimp

Siganus (səgānəs) — type genus of Family Siganidae, the rabbitfish

Signigobius ('signə,gōbēəs) — signal gobies, Family Gobidae, benthic species that mimic the appearance and movements of a crab; pairs are sometimes exhibited in minireef aquariums

silicone cement — an adhesive suitable for the manufacture of all glass aquarium tanks, the development of which in the 1960s made keeping marine aquariums feasible for home hobbyists for the first time

Sinularia ('sinyə,larēə) — an alcyonarian soft coral often maintained in minireef aquariums

siphon — suction created by the movement of water through a pipe in response to gravity, or to transfer water by means of such a pipe, or the pipe itself; also, a duct through which water enters or leaves the body of a mollusk

siphon

siphonoglyph (sī'fänə,glif) — a ciliated slit or groove leading to the mouth of a sea anemone

siphonoglyph

sipunculid ((')sī¦pəŋkyələd) — any worm of Phylum Sipunculida, a small marine group notable for the ability of some species to bore into rocks, and in which state they are often introduced into marine reef aquariums

sluff — to discard, as of dead skin

small-polyped stony (SPS) corals — those species in which the individual corallites are only a few millimeters in diameter, generally amenable to aquarium propagation by cutting up the colony into daughter colonies

snout length — the distance from the most anterior margin of the eye to the anterior end of the upper jaw

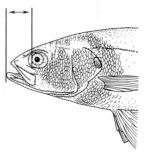

snout length

soft dorsal fin — one in which the rays are bilaterally paired, segmented structures usually branching one or more times toward the extremities

soft dorsal fin

soft rays — supporting fin elements that are bilaterally paired, segmented, and usually branching toward the extremities

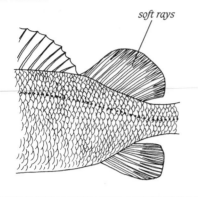

soft rays

soft water — water that has dissolved solids amounting to less than 100 parts per million

solubility — the tendency of a substance to form a solution, usually with water as the solute

Sorubim ('sōrübəm) — shovel-nosed catfish, Family Pimelodontidae, a predatory though docile species from the Amazon, Venezuela, and Paraguay

sparge — to discharge air or other gasses under pressure into a tank of water

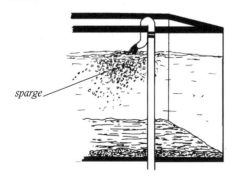

sparge

Spathiphyllum (spā'thə'fīləm) — flowering tropical plants of the *Arum* family forming rosettes of stiff, glossy leaves; sometimes included in fresh-water aquariums, although not truly aquatic

spawn — to release eggs and sperm into the surrounding water, or to engage in ritualized behavior associated with such release

spawning media — an artificial substrate for the deposition of fish eggs, varied according to the needs of a particular species

spawning mop — an arrangement of short filaments affixed to a float, intended as a substitute for floating vegetation into which fish will deposit eggs

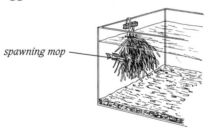

spawning mop

spawning plate — a piece of hard, flat material, such as slate, plastic, or glass intended as a substitute for a natural substrate onto which fish will deposit eggs

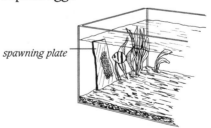

spawning plate

species — one or more genetically distinct populations of organisms that actually or potentially interbreed but are reproductively isolated from other such groups

Sphaeramia ('sfirəmēə) — cardinalfish, Family Apogonidae; the pajama cardinal, *S. nematoptera*, is regularly imported for marine aquariums

sphincter ('sfiŋ(k)tə(r)) — a muscular ring surrounding a body opening, permitting it to be opened and closed

spicule ('spi,kyül) — a microscopic structural element, of silica, lime, or protein, found in several plant and invertebrate groups and sometimes useful for the identification of taxa

spinous dorsal fin — one in which the supporting elements are solid, unpaired, and unsegmented

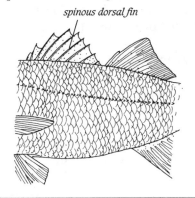

spinous dorsal fin

Spirobranchus ('spī(,)rō'braŋkəs) — Christmas tree worms, polychaete annelids of Family Serpulidae; exhibited in marine aquariums because of their brilliantly colored spiral radioles

that are immediately withdrawn into a protective tube at the slightest disturbance

spirocysts (,spīrə'sists) — a type of nematocyst from which a coiled filament is ejected

Spirographis (spī'rä'grafəs) — an Indo-Pacific serpulid worm exhibited in minireef aquariums because of its delicate white or pink radioles

sponge filter — one in which water is drawn through an element made of plastic foam, the pores of which trap particulate matter and provide a surface for the growth of nitrifying bacteria; useful as a temporary filter for small aquariums

standard length — the distance measured from the tip of the snout to the base of the tail

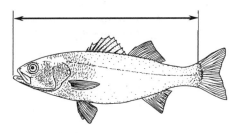

standard length

stand — a support for an aquarium tank, usually not enclosed below the tank

standpipe — a tube extending vertically from a drain, allowing the level of water in the container to rise, or "stand," above the level at which the drain exits

standpipe

stolon — a runner, or horizontal plant stem, that gives rise to a daughter plant at its tip, or any anatomical structure that resembles such a stem

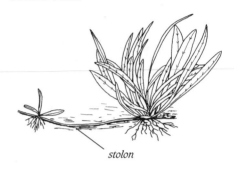

stolon

Steatocranus (‚stēəd·ə'kranəs) — cichlids from Central Africa bearing a fatty hump on the forehead; they are of interest to aquarists because they form lifelong sexual pairs

Stegastes (stə'gāstəs) — gregory or farmerfish, Family Pomacentridae; they cultivate algae upon branching coral heads within their territories by weeding out undesirable growth

Stenopus (stə̇nə'pəs) — barber shrimps, Family Stenopodidae, including the commonly imported species *S. hispidus*, the banded coral shrimp, and several other species that exhibit cleaning behavior

Stenorhynchus (stə̇nə'riŋkəs) — the arrow crab, *S. seticornis*, often collected in Florida for exhibition in home aquariums; it feeds on polychate worms and other small invertebrates

Stichodactyla (‚stikə'dakt³lə) — carpet anemones, at least three species of which are known in the marine aquarium trade; all host anemonefish are difficult for many hobbyists to maintain successfully

stoloniferan (‚stōlə'nif(ə)rən) — soft corals in which the individual polyps are connected by horizontal threads of tissue resembling stolons, including several species maintained in minireef aquariums

stonefish — scorpaenid fish, of the genus *Synancea*, bearing venomous spines; *S. verrucosa* has caused human fatalities; it should never be exhibited in a home aquarium

streptomycin (‚streptō'mīs³n) — an antibiotic derived from the actinomycete *Streptomyces*

Strombus ('strämbəs) — conchs, *S. gigas*, cultivated in the Caribbean for food and as algae eaters for the marine aquarium

Stylophora ('stīlə'f(ə)rə) — a small-polyped stony coral forming rounded colonies of finger branches, widely distributed in the Indo-Pacific and easily propagated in minireef aquariums

subcellular — having to do with anatomical structures smaller than a single cell, or those located within a cell

subcutaneous ('səb'kyü'tānēəs) — of the area just beneath the skin of an animal

submersible heater — an electrically operated device for raising the temperature of aquarium water that can be completely covered with water without creating a shock hazard

submersible heater

substrate — 1) the material placed on the bottom of an aquarium tank; 2) any surface to which a living organism attaches itself; 3) the particular compound acted upon by an enzyme

sump — a reservoir for water being transported by a pump

supernatant — the liquid phase above a sediment layer

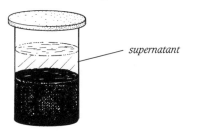

supernatant

surgeonfish — any of Family Acanthuridae, so called because of a bladelike modified scale, often retractable into a sheath on the caudal peduncle, that can deliver a serious cut

sustainable harvest — the removal of individuals from a habitat, in a manner and under such circumstances that permit the taking to continue without measurably reducing the size of the reproducing population of the target species, or upon other species, such as predators, that are ecologically related to the target species

sweeper tentacle — an elongated appendage produced by some stony corals that stings other organisms that move or grow too near the coral colony

swim bladder — a thin-walled, gas-filled sac found in bony fish that permits them to control their bouyancy and thus to rise or sink in the water column

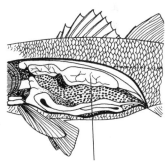

swim bladder

symbiont — any species characteristically found only in the presence of another

symbiosis — an ecological relationship between two different species; a symbiotic relationship

sympatric — said of species that occur in the same geographic location

Symphysodon (ˌsimˌfizˈsädən) — South American discus fish, cichlids in which parental care extends to the production of a skin exudate upon which the fry feed

symptom — any measurable evidence of a pathological condition, especially if employed in the diagnosis of such condition

Synalpheus (sinˌalfēəs) — snapping or popping shrimps, Family Alpheidae; they are able to make a loud "pop" by means of a specially modified chela

Synanceia (ˌsinˈans(y)ēə) — stonefish, potentially deadly scorpaenids

Synchiropus (ˈsiŋkeˌkärōpəs) — the target fish or spotted mandarin, Family Callonymidae, exhibited in minireef aquariums where it feeds only on tiny, living crustaceans

Syngnathus (ˈsiŋnəthəs) — pipefish, type genus of Family Syngnathidae

Synodontis (ˌsinəˈdäntəs) — type genus of the Family Synodontidae, African catfish including the upsidedown catfish

Taeniacra ('tēnēə̩akrə) — the black-striped dwarf cichlid of Brazil, *T. candidae*, a beautiful species maintained by cichlid enthusiasts

tank — the container, usually of glass or acrylic, that holds an aquarium

tankmate — any organism that shares an aquarium with another

taste buds — stuctures in the oral cavity of fish and other vertebrates in which nerve receptors sensitive to chemical conditions are located

taxon — any group into which species are arranged as part of a classification

taxonomic hierarchy — a logical series of successively larger groups into which a species may be placed according to its supposed evolutionary relationships with other species

taxonomist — a biologist primarily concerned with the identification of species and the elucidation of evolutionary relationships between them

taxonomy — the science of classification of species according to their evolutionary history

Tealia (tēlēə) — small sea anemones, often red in color, distributed circumtropically

teeth — the bony elements located in the jaws of vertebrates, or any analogous structures in invertebrate animals, used for piercing, cutting, or tearing food

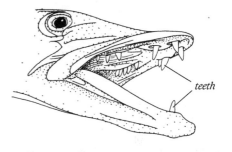

teeth

teleost ('tē̩läst) — a bony fish

Telmatactis (̩telmə'taktis) — a tiny sea anemone often carried by the boxing crab, *Lybia*

Telmatochromis (̩telmə'tō'krōməs) — a genus of cichlids endemic to Lake Tanganyika, Africa, including *T. temporalis*

telson — the tail flap, or terminal appendage, of the abdomen of a crustacean

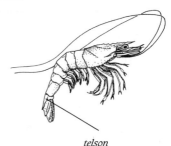

telson

tentacles — the appendages of certain animals, especially cnidarians and cephalopod mollusks, generally elongated, cylindrical, and with a sensory or food capture function or both

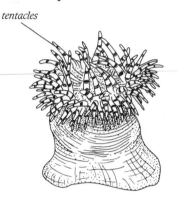

tentacles

terpenes ('tər͵pēns) — chemical compounds released by certain soft corals and thought to be inimical to competing species in the vicinity of the releasor

test — a protective integument comprised of calcified plates fused together

tetra — any of the characins, but especially the smaller species kept in freshwater community tanks

Tetraodon (te·'trāə͵dän) — type genus of Family Tetraodontidae, or puffers; the name refers to the presence of four incisor teeth

Thalassia (thə'lasēə) — turtle grass, a tropical marine flowering plant that forms large stands in shallow water

Thalassoma (͵thalə'sōmə) — wrasses, Family Labridae, including many aquarium species

thallus — the undifferentiated, leafless, and stemless body of a nonflowering plant, such as a seaweed or liverwort

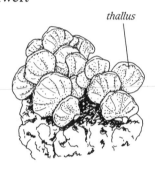

thallus

Thayeria ('thā'yərēə) — South American characins including the penguin tetra, *T. obliqua*, with a distinctive black stripe and a characteristic head-up swimming posture

thoracic (thə'rasik) — of the thorax or middle body area of a crustacean, or of the area enclosed by the rib cage of a vertebrate

threatened species — one of an officially recognized list of organisms in significant danger of extinction; but not to such a degree that a single catastrophic event could have this result

Tilapia (tə̇'lāpēə) — cichlids, native to central Africa, widely cultivated in aquariums and as food fish

titrant — a reagent used to neutralize an acid or base with the goal of determining the equivalency of the latter

toadfish — any of the marine fish in the genus *Opsanus*; easily maintained in aquariums because of their hardy nature and nonselective feeding habits

topping up — adding water to an aquarium to compensate for evaporation

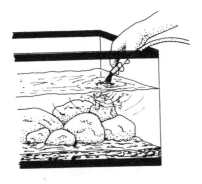

topping up

total hardness — the combined mass of carbonates of calcium and magnesium per unit volume of water

total length — the distance from the anterior extremity of the head to the posterior extremity of either lobe of the caudal fin

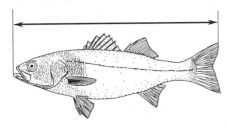

total length

toxin — any substance produced by one species that is harmful to other species that come into contact with it; a poison

Toxotes ('täksə,tēz) — archerfish, fresh- or brackish water species that obtain insects by knocking them from plants overhanging the water by means of a jet of water expelled forcefully from the fish's mouth

trace element — components of seawater present at a concentration of 1 part per billion or less

Trachyphyllia ('trakē,fil(y)ēə) — open brain coral, a large-polyped stony coral adapted for living in bottom sediments; easily maintained in minireef aquariums

transparent — allowing the free passage of light

transverse fission — splitting of a parent cell or organism along the short axis of the body into two daughter cells or organisms

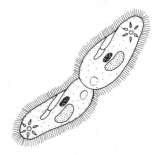

transverse fission

Trichogaster (trə'ko'gastər) — anabantids, such as the pearl gourami, in which the pectoral fins are modified into whiskerlike sensory appendages, and that reach an adult size greater than 3 inches (7.6 cm)

Trichopsis ('trikə,opsəs) — the three-striped croaking gourami, and related fish from Thailand noted for the ability to produce audible sounds

trickle filter — an aquarium water purification device in which tank water flows slowly, or trickles, over media not submerged but held in a tray or chamber, with the intent of facilitating attachment and growth of nitrifying bacteria

Tridachia (trə'dākēə) — a sea slug of the tropical Atlantic and Caribbean that is capable of removing the chloroplasts from the seaweeds upon which it feeds and transferring them to its own body where they continue to photosynthsize, thus providing the slug with food

Tridacna (trə'daknə) — giant clams cultivated primarily for food but also, because of their bright colors and ease of maintenance in minireef tanks, for the aquarium market

tridacnid (trə'daknid) — any of the mollusk Family Tridacnidae, or giant clams that feed by harboring photosynthetic unicellular algae within their mantle tissues

triggerfish — any marine species of Family Balistidae, characterized by dorsal and anal fin spines bearing a locking mechanism that allows the fish to wedge itself inextricably into a crevice or other space as a mode of defense

Tropheus (trō'fēəs) — colorful, aggressive cichlids endemic to Lake Tanganyika, Africa; widely maintained by specialized aquarists

trophic level — the position in a food web that a particular type of organism occupies

trophic level

tropical fish — those from any waters lying between the Tropic of Cancer and the Tropic of Capricorn, especially freshwater species imported for ornamental aquariums

trunk — that portion of the body of a fish between the head and the caudal region and containing the abdominal cavity

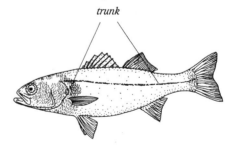

trunk

Tubastrea (tü'bəstrēə) — a non-photosynthetic stony coral sought after by enthusiasts because of its bright orange coloration

tubercle ('t(y)übə(r)kəl) — a bump or point arising from the body surface of an organism, especially such a structure on the head of a breeding male of certain fish species

tubeworm — any aquatic annelid that dwells within an elongate, hollow burrow or refuge it constructs or secretes and into which, typically, it is capable of withdrawing to escape danger

tube feet — external appendages of echinoderms, part of the water vascular system; they act like suction cups to allow the animal to grip the substrate or to capture prey

tube feet

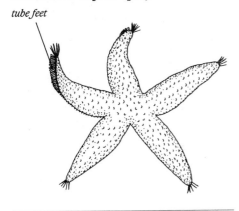

Tubifex ('t(y)übə,feks) — freshwater annelids widely collected for fish food, but now considered unsafe to feed because of their preference for organically polluted waters; also sold in freeze-dried form

Tubipora (t(y)ü'bē,porə) — the organ pipe "coral," a colonial hydrozoan that produces a calcified skeleton, deep maroon in color, superficially resembling that of a scleractinian

tunicate ('t(y)ünəkāt) — a urochordate, or sea squirt, the body of which is enclosed in a fleshy shroud, or "tunic," with two openings through which water is taken in and expelled

Turbinaria ('tərbə'nərēə) — cup coral, a stony coral with a skeleton resembling a wineglass, the inside of which is studded with corallites

Turbo — marine snails, Family Turbinidae, in which the shell resembles a turban; several species are used in marine aquariums for the control of filamentous and encrusting algae

U–V

Varu (yü'ru) — the waroo or triangle cichlid of the Amazon and Guyana, *U. amphiacanthoides*, a beautiful schooling species that is maintained with some difficulty by specialized aquarists

Udotea (yü'dōtēə) — green marine alga with a calcified skeletal structure giving it the shape of a fan emerging from the substrate

ultraviolet light (UV) — electromagnetic radiation with a wavelength between 100 and 380 nanometers

ultraviolet sterilization — elimination of microorganisms from water by exposure to ionizing light radiation

umbo (ü'mbō) — the oldest portion of the shell of a mollusk

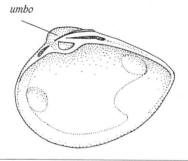

umbo

Umbra ('əmbrə) — mudminnows, Family Umbridae, native to North America and Eurasia; maintained successfully by aquarium hobbyists but rare and considered extinct in some portions of its natural range

undergravel filter — a device for enhancing bacterial nitrification in the substrate of an aquarium, consisting of a perforated plate upon which substrate is layered, through which water is drawn and expelled near the surface of the tank by various methods

undulipodium ('ənjə'līpōdēəm) — the long, whiplike locomotory organelle of a eukaryotic cell, synonymous with flagellum in common usage; the latter term is reserved by microbiologists for the functionally similar structure of a prokaryotic cell

undulipodium

urogenital opening (,yùrə¦jenəd·əl ōp,(ə)niŋ) — the common outlet of the excretory and reproductive systems in fish

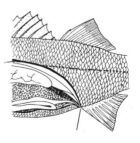

urogenital opening

uropod ('yūrə,päd) — the flattened blades of the sixth abdominal appendage of crustaceans, together with the telson forming a tail fin

uropod

Utricularia (yü·,trikyə'la(a)rēə) — bladderworts, freshwater flowering plants of temperate, tropical, and subtropical America with tiny bladders that trap microinvertebrates; maintained in aquariums and garden ponds as a curiosity

Valenciennea (və¦len(t)sē¦enēə) — marine sleeper gobies, Family Gobidae, that feed by taking substrate material into the mouth and extracting benthic microinvertebrates

Vallisneria (,valəs'nirēə) — eelgrass, freshwater temperate, tropical, and subtropical flowering plants with long, straplike leaves, many species of which are cultivated in aquariums

variegated — having leaves of more than one color, usually green and white

variegated

vegetarian — an organism whose diet contains no animal matter

ventral fin — an alternative name for the pelvic fin, or most posterior paired appendage of fish

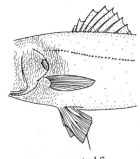

ventral fin

venturi (ven·'tūrē) — a device for injecting gas into a stream of water, consisting of a specially milled pipe that creates a pressure drop near an orifice, resulting in the intake of gas through that orifice

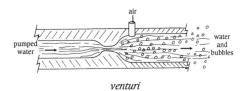

venturi

verrucae (və'rükē) — small bumps or raised areas on the column of an anemone, useful for identification

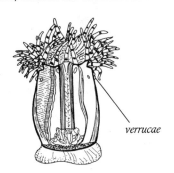

verrucae

vertebrate — an animal with a segmented, bony or cartilaginous spinal column, including fish, amphibians, reptiles, birds, and mammals

vesicle — a fluid-filled sac surrounded by tissue or a membrane

Vesicularia (və͵sikyə'la(a)rēə) — Java moss, *V. dubeyana*, an aquatic bryophyte maintained in freshwater aquariums

Vibrio ('vibrēō) — a gram-negative, curved, rod-shaped bacteria responsible for various pathogenic conditions in fish, amphibians, and other organisms

viscera ('visərə) — the internal organs of an animal

viviparous ((')vī͵vip(ə)rəs) — giving birth to living young

volute — the "head" of a water pump, with inlet and outlet openings, through which water is propelled by the movement of the impeller

vomer ('vōmə(r)) — a portion of the skull of teleost fish, sometimes bearing teeth, the structure of which is useful in taxonomy

water changes — the removal and replacement of old aquarium water with new

water changes

water chemistry — the measurement and evaluation of water parameters, or the present state of those parameters

water quality — the overall suitability of an aquarium's water for the organisms exhibited therein

water softener — any device or medium for reducing hardness, or the concentration of dissolved carbonates of calcium and magnesium in fresh water

wavemaker — an electrical device that enables timed switching of power between two or more pumps, with the aim of creating changing currents

Weber's apparatus — an anatomical structure found in characins and related fish that connects the auditory organs with the swim bladder, which, in turn, operates as a sounding board, giving the fish an especially keen sense of hearing

wet/dry filter — any device for enhancing bacterial nitrification in which the medium upon which bacteria attach is not submerged, but rather moistened by water pumped over or through it

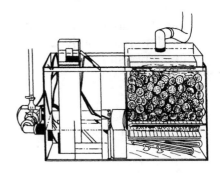

wet/dry filter

white band disease — a pathogenic condition of stony corals in which an area of dying tissue is preceded by a distinctive pale ring

wrasse ('ras) — any of the numerous species in the marine fish Family Labridae, with elongate body and large canine teeth

X-Y-Z

xanthophyll ('zan(t)thə,fil) — a yellow pigment produced by many plants and algae

Xenia ('zēnēə) — a stoloniferan soft coral often maintained in mini-reef aquariums; in some species the polyps pulse rhythmically

Xiphophorus (zə̇'fäfərəs) — live-bearers, Family Poecilidae, including both platies and swordtails, two of the most popular freshwater aquarium fish

yolk sac —a larval structure enclosing stored nutrients derived from the egg; in many fish it is retained for a period after hatching

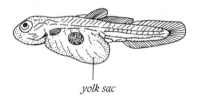

yolk sac

Zanclus ('zaŋkləs) — the Moorish idols, Family Zanclidae, marine fish related to acanthurids and often imported from Hawaii; extremely difficult to maintain in a home aquarium

Zebrasoma (zēbrə,sōmə) — acanthurids with elongate snouts suitable for picking filamentous algae from rocks; the genus includes many marine aquarium species, such as the yellow tang, *Z. flavescens*

zoanthid (zō'an(t)thə̇d) — any of the sea mats of the anthozoan Order Zoantharia, colonial polyps up to several inches in height, usually interconnected at the base by a sheet of tissue and lacking a skeleton; often exhibited in minireef aquariums

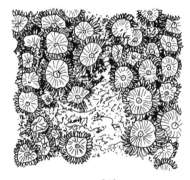

zoanthid

Zoanthus (zō'an(t)thəs) — the genus of zoanthids most commonly seen in the aquarium trade

zonation — patterns of colonization of a habitat by living organisms, depending upon specific conditions, such as the degree of exposure at low tide or altitude

zoochlorellae (¦zōə,klə'relā) — green algae living in mutualistic symbiosis with certain invertebrates, ranging from the freshwater *Hydra* to marine organisms such as tunicates and sponges

zoogeography — the study of the spatial distribution of species

zooplankton — nonphotosynthetic organisms suspended or swimming in the water column, often feeding on phytoplankton and, in turn, providing food for a variety of larger organisms

zooxanthellae (ˌzōəzanˈthələ) — dinoflagellates living in mutualistic symbiosis with certain invertebrates, including many species of cnidarians and mollusks kept in minireef aquariums; they are of critical importance in the physiology of reef-building stony corals (*see* DINOFLAGELLATE)

COLOR
PHOTO
GALLERY

Live plants, such as the easily grown Java Fern, *Microsorium pteropus*, need sufficient light and proper water quality to thrive.

Reef aquariums usually feature live rock, typically encrusted with lovely mauve and purple coralline algae.

Among the several species of suckermouth catfishes, the Royal Panaque, *Panaque nigrolineatus*, is possibly the most attractive.

Like all labyrinth fish, the male Siamese Fighting Fish, *Betta splendens*, builds a floating bubble nest.

Humbugs, such as *Dascyllus melanurus*, are among the hardiest of marine fish, and can be recommended even for beginners.

Tubeworms, like these *Protula magnifica*, are kept by hobbyists intrigued by their feathery feeding structures, the radioles.

The Angelfish, *Pterophyllum scalare*, has been bred to create aquarium varieties such as this magnificent pair with marbled coloration.

For a beautiful community aquarium, choose an assortment of fish whose colors are complementary.

The Dragon Moray Eel, *Muraena pardalis*, feeds mostly on other marine fish, aided by its many sharp teeth.

Small, colorful sea stars, such as *Fromia nodosa*, make excellent aquarium inhabitants.

Microgeophagus ramirezi, known as the Dwarf Ram Cichlid, is a favorite member of the vast cichlid family.

The Scarlet Lady Shrimp, *Lysmata amboiensis*, is a popular example of a shrimp that exhibits cleaning behavior, removing parasites and dead tissue from fishes.

The Guppy, *Poecilia reticulata*, has been bred to create numerous aquarium varieties, such as this male "flametail" type.

The most commonly available of the scats, *Scatophagus argus*, lives in brackish water.

Barbus titteya, the Cherry Barb, can be easily maintained in a small community aquarium.

Few species can top the Red Wag Platy, *Xiphophorus maculatus*, for coloration and ease of aquarium care.

Corydoras julii, hardy and commonly available, is a good catfish for the community tank.

The red color form of the Oscar, *Astronotus ocellatus*, does well in a large aquarium by itself.

Monos, including *Monodactylus sebae*, may be successfully maintained in either marine or brackish water.

Groupers are marine fish that lie in wait, using their large mouth to swallow their prey whole, as this Coral Grouper, *Cephalopholis miniatus*, demonstrates.

A school of the Red Serpae Tetra, *Hyphessobrycon serpae*, with Amazon sword plants, *Echinodorus*.

Phractocephalus hemiliopteris, the Redtail Catfish, will outgrow any but the largest aquarium tank.

The male Red Gularis, *Aphyosemion sjoestedti*, is likely to fight with other male killifish in the same aquarium.

Family Mastacembelidae, the spiny eels, includes many interesting species that adapt well to the aquarium, like this *Macrognathus aculeatus* specimen.

Carefully chosen plastic plants can deceive the observer, looking quite naturalistic.

Several species of the large goby clan, including the Red Headed Goby, *Gobiosoma (Elactinus) puncticulatus*, are produced in marine fish hatcheries.

The Longnosed Hawkfish, *Oxycirrhites typus*, like others in its family, is often found perched on a coral head.

Clownfish, like *Amphiprion percula*, live in symbiotic association with giant sea anemones, but need not have an anemone present in the aquarium.

Tridacna maxima and several other species of giant clams are cultivated for the coloration of their mantle tissues.

Dwarf angelfish, typified by *Centropyge bispinosus*, the Coral Beauty, are more easily maintained than their larger cousins.

African cichlids are usually maintained in community aquariums featuring lots of rocks; plastic plants survive the digging activities of the fish.

Although commonly called "freshwater puffers," these fish, such as *Tetraodon nigroveridis*, should have water that is somewhat salty.

The delicate Pencilfish, *Nannostomus eques*, does best in a planted aquarium.

Gouramis, like the Blue Gourami, *Trichogaster trichopterus*, are also available in golden and opaline color varieties.

Among the danios, *Danio aequipinnatus*, grows largest and so is called the Giant Danio.

Brightly colored males, typified by Foersch's Killifish, *Nothobranchius foerschi*, are the main attraction of the killifish family.

Most blennies, including *Istiblennius chrysospilos*, have "eyebrows" and a droll expression.

The green coloration of this Open Brain Coral, *Trachyphyllia geoffreyi*, is one indication of its need for light.

Bumblebee Gobies, *Brachygobius doriae*, need brackish water and live food to do their best in the aquarium.

Trichogaster leeri, the Pearl Gourami, is a peaceful, larger fish for the community aquarium.

Whiptail catfish, such as *Rineloricaria hasemani* shown here, feed on algae and must have driftwood on which to cling.

The Cardinal Tetra, *Paracheirodon axelrodi*, is available only seasonally, because it is collected from the wild.

Melanotaenia parkinsoni typifies the colorful, fast-swimming rainbowfish family.

Although numerous species of cichlids are found in Africa's rift lakes, *Melanochromis auratus* is among the most popular and widely available ones.

The popular Clown Loach, *Botia macracanthus*, resembles a catfish, but is related to barbs and other cyprinids.

Snakeheads, such as *Channa micropeltes*, are vicious predators that should be given a tank to themselves.

Fairy basslets, or anthias, live in groups dominated by a colorful male, such as this *Pseudanthias pleurotaenia*, or Square Block Anthias.

The Pajama Cardinalfish, *Sphaeramia nematoptera*, is active at night as are most other members of Family Apogonidae.

Bubble Coral, *Plerogyra sinuosa*, is a suitable species for the beginning hobbyist interested in a reef aquarium.

Scorpionfish, including *Pterois volitans*, the Lionfish, have venomous spines and must be handled with caution.

The Emperor Tetra, *Nematobrycon palmeri*, reaches nearly 3 inches (8 cm) in length.

Pike cichlids, such as *Crenicichla cyclostoma*, are predators not to be trusted with smaller fish.

Few marine fish can rival the herbivorous Yellow Tang, *Zebrasoma flavescens*, in popularity with hobbyists.

Leather corals, typified by *Sarcophyton trocheliophorum*, are popular and hardy subjects for the reef tank.

African cichlids often hybridize, creating interesting forms such as this *Pseudotropheus*.

The Tiger Barb, *Barbus tetrazona*, is apt to nip fins unless maintained in a group.

APPENDICES

1. MEASUREMENTS, EQUIVALENTS, AND FORMULAS

ELECTRICITY

watts = volts × amps
amps = volts/watts
1 amp = 120 watts at 120 volts
30 amp line capacity = 3,600 watts (30 × 120)
20 amp line capacity = 2,400 watts (20 × 120)
15 amp line capacity = 1,800 watts (15 × 120)

VOLUME

1 gallon = 3.785 L (liter)
= 3,785 cc (cubic centimeter)
= 3,785 ml (milliliter)

1 liter = 1,000 ml
= 1,000 cc
= 0.264 gal
= 35.28 oz (weight)
= 33.8 fluid oz
= 2.25 lb
= 1 kg water
cc = ml
drop = 1/20 ml
ml = 20 drops
tsp = 5 ml
tbsp = 15 ml
fl. oz = 30 ml

Aquarium capacity (gal) = L × W × H (inches)/231
(liters) = L × W × H (cm)/1,000
(liters to gal) = × 0.264

CONCENTRATIONS

parts per thousand (0/00 or ppt) = ml/L (liter)
= 3.8 ml/gal
= 3.8 gm/gal
= gm/1,000 gms
= gm/kilogram (Kg)
= gm/2.2 lbs
part per million (ppm) = mg/L
= 3.8 mg/gal
= gm/cubic meter of water
= ml/1,000 L
1 percent solution = 38 gm/gal
= 38 ml/gal
= 1 oz/3 quarts
= 1.3 oz/gal
= 10 gm/L
= 1 gm/100 ml
= 10 ml/L

1:1,000 solution = 1 ml/L
= 0.1 gm/100 ml
= 3.8 gm/gal
= 3.8 ml/gal
= 0.13 oz/gal

TEMPERATURE

Centigrade or Celsius = $(F - 32) \times 0.55$
Farenheit = $(C \times 1.8) + 32$

DISSOLVED GASES

Oxygen in ppm $\times$ 0.7 = O_2 in cc/L or ml/L
Oxygen in ml/L or cc/L $\times$ 1.429 = O_2 in ppm

CO_2 in ppm $\times$ 0.509 = CO_2 in ml/L or cc/L
CO_2 in cc/L or ml/L $\times$ 1.964 = CO_2 in ppm

APPENDICES

LOGARITHM TO THE BASE 10 PREFIX TERMS

billion	10^9	(G)	giga	1,000,000,000
million	10^6	(M)	mega	1,000,000
thousand	10^3	(k)	kilo	1,000
hundred	10^2	(h)	hecto	100
ten	10	(dk)	deka	10
(tenth)	10^{-1}	(d)	deci	0.1
(hundredth)	10^{-2}	(c)	centi	0.01
(thousandth)	10^{-3}	(m)	milli	0.001
(millionth)	10^{-6}	(μ)	micro	0.000001
(billionth)	10^{-9}	(n)	nano	0.000000001
(trillionth)	10^{-12}	(p)	pico	0.000000000001

ALKALINITY AND WATER HARDNESS

Several synonyms for "alkalinity" are used in the aquarium literature. Alkalinity is expressed in milliequivalents per liter (meq/L). Other terms used are "carbonate hardness" expressed in parts per million (ppm) or grains per gallon (gr/gal) of calcium carbonate, and "German hardness" or "KH," expressed in degrees (dKH). The relationships among these units are:

1 meq/L = 50 ppm $CaCO_3$ = 2.92 gr/gal $CaCO_3$ = 2.8 dKH

Descriptive terms for water hardness found in aquarium literature are subject to varying interpretation. We have indicated approximate ranges of hardness corresponding to each term.

very soft = <4 dKH or <75 ppm $CaCO_3$
soft = 5–8 dKH or 80–150 ppm $CaCO_3$
medium hard = 9–12 dKH or 160–220 ppm $CaCO_3$
hard = 13–20 dKH or 230–360 ppm $CaCO_3$
very hard = >20 dKH or >360 ppm $CaCO_3$

LIGHT INTENSITY

1 lumen = 1 footcandle
1 lux = 1 lumen/square meter

LENGTH

1 micron = 0.001 millimeter
1 millimeter = 0.001 meter = 0.039 inches
1 centimeter = 0.01 meter = 0.39 inches
1 meter = 39.37 inches = 3.28 feet
1 foot = 30.48 centimeters = 0.3 meters
1 yard = 3 feet = 0.91 meters

SURFACE AREA

1 square centimeter = 0.16 square inches
1 square meter = 10.76 square feet = 1.2 square yards
1 square inch = 6.45 square centimeters
1 square foot = 144 square inches = 0.09 square meters
1 square yard = 9 square feet = .81 square meters

WEIGHT

1 milligram = 0.001 grams
1 gram = 1000 milligrams = 0.035 ounces
1 kilogram = 1000 grams = 35 ounces = 2.2 pounds
1 ounce = 28.35 grams
1 pound = 16 ounces = 454 grams = 0.45 kilograms

OTHER DATA

1 gallon of fresh water weighs 8 pounds
1 gallon of sea water weighs 8.5 pounds
1 cubic foot of water = 7.5 gallons = 37.8 liters

2. CONVERSION OF OBSERVED HYDROMETER READINGS TO SALINITY

ESTIMATING SALINITY FROM OBSERVED HYDROMETER READING

Using a hydrometer, the salinity of the water can be calculated if the temperature is also known.

First, convert the temperature to Celsius, by using the following formula:

$$°C = 0.56 (°F - 32)$$

Next, read across to find the temperature in Table 1, and then read down in that column to the row corresponding to the observed hydrometer reading. The number in the table is a conversion factor, which should be added to the observed hydrometer reading. The result is the density of the water.

Table 1: Conversion of Observed Hydrometer Readings to Density

Observed Hydrometer Reading	20°	21°	22°	23°	24°	25°	26°
1.0170	10	12	15	17	20	22	25
1.0180	10	12	15	17	20	23	25
1.0190	10	12	15	18	20	23	26
1.0200	10	13	15	18	20	23	26
1.0210	10	13	15	18	21	23	26
1.0220	11	13	15	18	21	23	26
1.0230	11	13	16	18	21	24	26
1.0240	11	13	16	18	21	24	27
1.0250	11	13	16	18	21	24	27
1.0260	11	13	16	19	22	24	27
1.0270	11	14	16	19	22	24	27
1.0280	11	14	16	19	22	25	28
1.0290	11	14	16	19	22		

Finally, using Table 2, look up the salinity that corresponds to the density you just calculated.

Table 2: Conversion of Density to Salinity

Density	Salinity	Density	Salinity	Density	Salinity
1.0180	25	1.0225	30	1.0270	36
1.0185	25	1.0230	31	1.0275	37
1.0190	26	1.0235	32	1.0280	38
1.0195	27	1.0240	32	1.0285	38
1.0200	27	1.0245	33	1.0290	39
1.0205	28	1.0250	34	1.0295	40
1.0210	29	1.0255	34	1.0300	40
1.0215	29	1.0260	35		
1.0220	30	1.0265	36		

Natural salinity is 35 in the vicinity of most coral reefs, unless the ocean is diluted from a nearby freshwater source. The acceptable range for invertebrates is 34 to 36, while fishes can tolerate lower salinities.

3. RECOMMENDED AQUARIUM ENVIRONMENTAL PARAMETERS

Freshwater. Freshwater environments are extremely diverse and the values given may be applicable only to certain habitats within the geographic area. Most common freshwater tropical fish available in pet shops do well in moderately hard, neutral to slightly acid water at temperatures of 70–80°F (21–26.7°C). However, providing the conditions found in the natural environment of any species will result in healthier fish, and is often essential for successful breeding. Always consult references for precise information regarding the needs of the species you intend to keep.

South America (characins, dwarf cichlids, angelfish, discus, many catfish)

```
Hardness    — < 1.0–7 dKH          ⎫
pH          — 5.0–7.2              ⎬ depending upon species
Temperature — 72–80°F (22–26.7°C)  ⎭
```

Central America (live-bearing toothed carps, many larger cichlids, catfish)

```
Hardness    — 9–20 dKH (live-bearers),   ⎫ depending upon
              5–8 dKH (cichlids)         ⎪ species (often cooler
pH          — 7.0–7.5 (live-bearers),    ⎬ for live-bearers,
              6.5–7.0 (cichlids)         ⎪ warmer for cichlids)
Temperature — 70–80°F (21–26.7°C)        ⎭
```

Africa (central and western rivers: characins, cichlids, barbs)

```
Hardness    — 2–3 dKH
pH          — 6.5
Temperature — 80°F (26.7°C)
```

Africa (eastern lakes: mouthbrooding cichlids and catfish)

```
Hardness    — 10–17 dKH
pH          — > 8.0
Temperature — 80°F (26.7°C)
```

Southeast Asia (danios, rasboras, barbs, loaches, labyrinth fish)

Hardness — < 1.0 dKH
pH — 6.0
Temperature — 72–82°F (22.2–28°C)
} depending upon species (many of these are among the hardiest, most adaptable aquarium fish)

North America (sunfish, percids, catfish)

Hardness — 12–20 dKH
pH — 5.5–8.5
Temperature — 65–75°F (18.3–23.9°C)
} depending upon species

Brackish Water. Brackish-water environments occur where a freshwater river meets the salt water of the ocean. Because such areas are often subject to fluctuations in conditions, fish living here can tolerate a wide range. The parameters suggested below are therefore average conditons. Always consult references for precise information regarding the needs of the species you intend to keep.

Salinity — 15–20 ppt (can range from 0 to full strength seawater, 35 ppt)
pH — 8.0
Temperature — 72–80°F (22.2–26.7°C)

Marine. Marine environments are extremely stable. Most of the fish and invertebrates maintained in aquariums come from coral reefs or adjacent habitats; thus, the aquarium conditions they require are similar. Fish, generally, will tolerate lowered salinities and lower temperatures than invertebrates will, but all do best if maintained at the parameters indicated. Species from temperate waters, such as the Atlantic coast of the United States, must have cooler temperatures but the same chemical conditions as those from the tropics.

Temperature — 74–82°F (23–28°C) for tropical species,
60–72°F (15.5–22°C) for temperate species
Salinity — 34–36 ppt
pH — 8.15–8.6 (8.2–8.3 optimum)
Alkalinity — 2.0–5. 0 meq/L (6–15 dKH)
Ammonia (NH_3) — Zero
Nitrite (NO_{2-}) — Zero

Nitrate (NO_3-) — < 20 mg/L (nitrate ion) =
< 4.55 mg/L (nitrogen as nitrate)

Phosphate (PO_4^{-3}) — < 0.05 mg/L

Calcium (Ca^{+2}) — 375–475 mg/L

Strontium (Sr^{+2}) — 8.0 mg/L

Iodide (I^-) — 0.6 mg/L

Dissolved Oxygen (O_2) — > 6.90 mg/L

4. DIRECTORY OF ORGANIZATIONS, SOCIETIES, AND PERIODICALS

ORGANIZATIONS

The listing is alphabetical. If the organization publishes a journal or other periodical, we have given its name in italics in parentheses below the name of the organization. Other listed organizations may publish a newsletter for members. Some of the groups listed have membership restrictions, but most welcome any participation. Hobbyist societies are listed in the next section.

Any organization or publisher wishing to update its information in future editions of this book is urged to notify the author by writing in care of the publisher, or by sending e-mail to: **ichthystn@hotmail.com**

American Marinelife Dealers Association
(*Marinelife Dealer*)
569 32 Road STE 7B #241
Grand Junction, CO 81504

Aquarium Systems, Inc.
(*SeaScope*)
8141 Tyler Boulevard
Mento, OH 44060

The Aquatic Gardener
6205 Lookout Loop
Raleigh, NC 27612

Breeder's Registry
(*Journal of Maquaculture*)
P.O. Box 255373
Sacramento, CA 95865
breeders@kplace.monrou.com

Center for Marine Conservation
1725 De Sales Street NW
Washington, DC 20036

The Cousteau Society
870 Greenbriar Circle, Suite 402
Chesapeake, VA 23320-2641
cousteau@infi.net

Coral Reef Alliance
809 Delaware Street
Berkeley, CA 94710
CoralReefA@aol.com

EMAP Pursuit Publishing
(*Practical Fishkeeping*)
Bretton Court
Bretton, Peterborough
PE3 8DZ United Kingdom

Fancy Publications
(*Aquarium Fish Magazine, Pet Product News*)
P.O. Box 6050
Mission Viejo, CA 92690

International Center for Living Aquatic Resources Management
MCPO Box 2361
0718 Makati M.M.
Philippines
j.mcmanus@cgnet.com

International Coral Reef Initiative, OES/ETC
Room 4325
2201 C Street NW
Washington, DC 20520
sdrake@state.gov

International Marinelife Alliance
2335 Murilla Way S.
St. Petersburg, FL 33712

International Society for Reef Studies
(*Coral Reef, Reef Encounter*)
Dr. John Ogden
Florida Institute of Oceanography
830 First Street S
St. Petersburg, FL 33701

Ocean Realm
4067 Broadway
San Antonio, TX 78209

Ocean Voice International
10 Henri Lassard
Pt. Gatineau, PQ
J8T 3G6 Canada

Ornamental Fish International
(*OFI Journal*)
Apartado de Correos 129
29692 Sabinillas
Manilva, Malaga, Spain

Pet Dealer
2 University Plaza, Suite #11
Hackensack, NJ 07601

Pet Industry Joint Advisory Council
1220 19th St. NW Suite 400
Washington, DC 20036

RCM Publications
(*Freshwater and Marine Aquarium Magazine*)
144 West Sierra Madre Boulevard
Sierra Madre, CA 91024

TFH Publications, Inc.
(*Tropical Fish Hobbyist*)
One TFH Plaza
Neptune, NJ 07753

University of Hawaii Sea Grant College Program
(*Makai*)
1000 Pope Road, Room 200
Honolulu, HI 96822

HOBBYIST SOCIETIES

The benefits of joining an aquarium club or society are many. If possible, join a local club to learn more about aquarium keeping, and also join a specialty society, if you have a particular interest. If there is no club in your area, consider starting one with a group of aquarist friends. Most clubs and specialty societies have informative newsletters, and many sponsor annual fish shows or a convention.

Aquarium clubs change membership chairpersons and addresses for a variety of reasons. We regret any incorrect information.

Any society wishing to add or update its information in future editions of this book is urged to notify the author by writing in care of the publisher, or by sending e-mail to: **ichthystn@hotmail.com**

American Cichlid Association
ACA Membership Chair
P.O. Box 5351
Naperville, IL 60567-5351

APPENDICES

American Killifish Association
3084 East Empire Avenue
Benton Harbor, MI 49022-9718
rivulus@compuserve.com

American Livebearer Association
Membership Chairman
5 Zerbe Street
Cresonna, PA 17929-1513

Apistogramma Study Group
P.O. Box 504
Elkhorn, WI 53121

Aquatic Gardeners Association
Membership
71 Ring Road
Plympton, MA 02367

Atlanta Marine Aquarium Society
2180 Pleasant Hill Road #A5/188
Duluth, GA 30136

Betta and Anabantid Society of America
Membership Chair
P.O. Box 163811
Miami, FL 33116-3811

Boston Aquarium Society
255 Central St.
Boston, MA 01746

Brooklyn Aquarium Society
P.O. Box 290610
Brooklyn, NY 11229

Bucks County Aquarium Society
1668 Hatboro Road
Richboro, PA 18954

British Cichlid Association
Publicity Officer
70 Morton Street
Middleton, Manchester
M24 6AY United Kingdom

British Killifish Association
Membership Information
14 Hubbard Close
Wymondham, Norfolk
NR18 ODU United Kingdom

Canadian Society of Aquarium Clubs
95 East 31st Street
Hamilton, ON
L8V 3N9 Canada

Canadian Killifish Association
Membership Chair
1251 Bray Court
Mississauga, ON
L5J 3S4 Canada

Chicagoland Marine Aquarium Society
1455 Nottingham Lane
Hoffman Estates, IL 60195

Cichlasoma Study Group
Membership Chair
1813 Locks Mill Drive
Fenton, MO 63026-2662

Cleveland Saltwater Enthusiasts Association
20897 Fairpark Drive
Fairview Park, OH 44126

Dallas/Fort Worth Marine Aquarium Society
940 Eagle Drive
DeSoto, TX 75115

Desert Marine Society
P.O. Box 55642
Phoenix, AZ 85078

Federation of American Aquarium Societies
Membership Information
4816 East 64th Street
Indianapolis, IN 46220-4828

Florida Marine Aquarium Society
3280 South Miami Avenue
Miami, FL 33129

Goldfish Society of America
Membership Information
9107 West 154th Street
Prior Lake, MN 55372-2119

International Aquarium Societies
(Angelfish Study Group, Seahorse Keepers Society, IAS International Group, Online Hobbyist)
P.O. Box 373
Maine, NY 13802

International Betta Congress
Membership Chair
923 Wadsworth Street
Syracuse, NY 13208

APPENDICES

International Fancy Guppy Association
Membership Chair
Rt. 1, Box 166
Rustburg, VA 24588

International Marine Aquarist Association
Membership Secretary
27 Arlesey Road
Henlow, Bedfordshire
SG16 6DF United Kingdom

Kansas City Marine Club
512 Fillmore, Apt. #1
Topeka, KS 66606

Louisville Marine Aquarium Society
3112 Meadowlark Avenue
Louisville, KY 40213

Marine Aquarium Societies of North America
1426 Hidden River Road
Horse Cave, KY 42749

Marine Aquarium Society of Palm Beach
2409 S. Haverhill Road
West Palm Beach, FL 33415

Marine Aquarium Society of Los Angeles
21915 Wyandotte Street, Suite 120
Canoga Park, CA 91303

Marine Aquarium Society of Memphis
P.O. Box 241282
Memphis, TN 38124

APPENDICES

Marine Aquarium Society of Michigan
1090 Dye Krest Drive
Flint, MI 48532

Marine Aquarium Society of Toronto
22 Quail Valley Drive
Thornhill, ON
L3T 4R2 Canada

Marine Aquarium Society of Virginia
P.O. Box 34392
Richmond, VA 23234

North American Fish Breeders Guild
Membership Information
RR # 2, Box 67-L
Orangeville, PA 17859
onsiteina@juno.com

North American Discus Society
Membership Information
6939 Justine Drive
Mississauga, ON
L4T 1M4 Canada

North American Native Fishes Association
P.O. Box 2304
Kensington, MD 20891

Pittsburgh Marine Aquarist Society
5901 Elgin Street
Pittsburgh, PA 15206

SEABay (Saltwater Enthusiasts Association of the Bay Area)
27066 Columbia Court
Hayward, CA 94542

Tampa Bay Aquarium Society
10424 Tara Drive
Riverview, FL 33569

Wasatch Marine Aquarium Society
6031 Loder Drive
Kearns, UT 84118

5. PUBLIC AQUARIUMS

Public aquariums are great places to see fish, including species you cannot keep at home—"up close and personal." They are also good sources of ideas for your home tank. Most important, their professional staffs are usually more than willing to assist an amateur with technical advice. Many public aquariums are members of the American Zoo and Aquarium Association. To search its membership directory, visit *www.aza.org/members/zoo*. Individual aquariums also have web sites.

Aquarium for Wildlife Conservation
(formerly New York Aquarium)
Boardwalk at West 8th Street
Brooklyn, NY 11224

Dallas Aquarium Fair Park
1462 First Avenue
Dallas, TX 75226

Monterey Bay Aquarium
886 Cannery Row
Monterey, CA 93940

National Aquarium in Baltimore
Pier Three
Baltimore, MD 21202

New England Aquarium
Central Wharf
Boston, MA 01701

Scripps Institution of Oceanography
Scripps Aquarium-Museum
La Jolla, CA 92093

Shedd Aquarium
1200 South Lake Shore Dr.
Chicago, IL 60605

Smithsonian Institution
Museum of Natural History
Marine Ecosystems
Washington, DC 20560

Tennessee Aquarium
1 Broad Street
Chattanooga, TN 37401

Vancouver Public Aquarium
P.O. Box 3232
Vancouver, BC
V6B 3X8 Canada

Waikiki Aquarium
2777 Kalakaua Ave.
Honolulu, HI 96815

6. AQUARIUM-RELATED SITES
ON THE INTERNET

This is only a partial list. Many of the web sites in the following list have additional links to other sites of interest. URLs were verified as of July, 1999, but are subject to change.

For subscribers to America Online:

Keyword AQUARIUM provides links to major public aquarium web sites.

Go to Keyword HOBBIES, then select "Aquarium Science" from the menu to access the aquarium hobby message board.

For subscribers to CompuServe Information Service:

GO FISHNET accesses the huge forum for aquarists, both freshwater and marine, including a library of indispensible information on a host of topics.

Other sites to visit using any web browser:

American Livebearer Association
http://www.petsforum.com/ala

American Marinelife Dealers Association
http://www.amdareef.com

American Zoos and Aquariums
http://www.aza.org

Apistogramma Study Group
http://user.me.net/~warewolf/apisto.html

Aquarium Frontiers Online
http://www.aquariumfrontiers.com/default.asp

Breeder's Registry
http://www.actwin.com/fish/br/index.html

Canadian Killifish Association
http://www.CKA.org

APPENDICES

Center for Marine Conservation
http://www.cmc-ocean.org

Conservation Fisheries
http://www.aquatic-specialists.com/cfi

Coral Reef Alliance
http://www.coral.org

Coral Reef Task Force
http://coralreef.gov/trade.html

Fish Information Service (FINS)
http://www.actwin.com/fish/index.html

International Aquarium Societies
http://www.spectra.net/~silvah/aquarium/aquahome.htm

International Marinelife Alliance
http://www.imamarinelife.org/

International Union for the Conservation of Nature
www.iucn.org

North American Native Fishes Association
http://www.nanfa.org

Online Reef Aquarist Society
http://www. panix.com/~cmo1/reef/

Pet Industry Joint Advisory Council
http://www.pijac.org

PGI Internet Service Center
http://www.petsforum.com

Project Seahorse
http://www.seahorse.mcgill.ca/

Reeflink
http://www.reeflink.com

Seahorse Research Society
http://members.aol.com/gatesma/private/Seahorse/index.html

Smithsonian Institution
http://seawiffs.gsfc.nasa.gov/ocean-planet.html

Virtual Pet Office Building
http://www.petsforum.com/petsforum/VPOB/

Waikiki Aquarium
http://www.mic.hawaii.edu/aquarium

Woods Hole Marine Biological Laboratory
http://www.mbl.edu/

The science of taxonomy, concerned with discovering and describing the enormous diversity of living organisms, is an ever-changing field. As research sheds light on species and their relationships, taxonomy—the categories of which ideally reflect the diverging paths taken by evolution—responds with name changes and the reassembly of families, orders, classes, phyla, kingdoms, and domains. Among aquarium organisms, fish, cnidarians, and arthropods are examples of taxa undergoing extensive revisions and ongoing research. Among numerous other groups, including in particular tiny or microscopic creatures that are important components of natural ecosystems as well as aquarium communities, knowledge of their ecology is so scant as to virtually guarantee extensive taxonomic revisions in the future.

Aquarists with an interest in taxonomy could hardly choose a better place to start than the University of Arizona's "Tree of Life" web site:

http://ag.arizona.edu/tree/phylogeny.html

This site also contains a links page:

http://ag.arizona.edu/tree/home.pages/links.html

that aquarists can use to ferret out sites devoted to a variety of specialized taxonomic interests.

Newsgroups

news.alt.aquaria

news.rec.aquaria

news.sci.aquaria

SELECTED BIBLIOGRAPHY

Adey, Walter H. and Karen Loveland. *Dynamic Aquaria*. New York: Academic Press, 1991.

Allen, Gerald R. *The Anemonefishes of the World; Species, Care and Breeding*. Mentor, OH: Aquarium Systems, 1980.

_____ and Roger C. Steene. *Reef Fishes of the Indian Ocean*. Neptune, NJ: TFH Publications, Inc., 1987.

_____ and Roger C. Steene. *Indo-Pacific Coral Reef Field Guide*. Singapore: Tropical Reef Research, 1994.

Amano, Tokashi. *Nature Aquarium World*. Neptune, NJ: TFH Publications, Inc., 1994.

Axelrod, H. R., W. E. Burgess, and C. W. Emmens. *Exotic Marine Fishes*. Neptune, NJ: TFH Publications, Inc., 1985. Looseleaf edition with supplements.

_____ and W. E. Burgess. *Saltwater Aquarium Fishes*. Neptune, NJ: TFH Publications, Inc., 1985.

Baensch, H. A. and R. Riehl. *Aquarium Atlas. Volume 2*. English edition. Shelburne, VT: Microcosm, 1997.

Barnes, R. D. *Invertebrate Zoology. 3rd ed.* Philadelphia, PA: W. B. Saunders, 1974.

Bearman, Gerry, ed. *Seawater, Its Composition, Properties, and Behaviour*. New York: Pergamon Press, 1989.

Bold, H. C. and M. J. Wynne. *Introduction to the Algae*. Englewood Cliffs, NJ: Prentice-Hall, 1978.

Bruner, Gerhard. *Aquarium Plants*. Neptune, NJ: TFH Publications, Inc., 1973.

Colin, P. L. *Caribbean Reef Invertebrates and Plants.* Neptune, NJ: TFH Publications, Inc., 1978.

Curtis, Helena. *Biology. 4th ed.* New York: Worth Publishing, 1983.

Debelius, Helmut. *Fishes for the Invertebrate Aquarium.* Mentor, OH: Aquarium Systems, 1989.

_____ and H. A. Baensch. *Marine Atlas 1.* English edition. Shelburne, VT: Microcosm, 1994.

Delbeek, J. C. and J. Sprung. *The Reef Aquarium, Volume I.* Coconut Grove, FL: Ricordea Publishing, 1994.

Erhardt, H. and H. Moosleitner. *Marine Atlas 2: Invertebrates.* English edition. Shelburne, VT: Microcosm, 1997.

_____. *Marine Atlas 3: Invertebrates.* English edition. Shelburne, VT: Microcosm, 1998.

Etnier, D. A. and W. C. Starnes. *The Fishes of Tennessee.* Knoxville, TN: The University of Tennessee Press, 1993.

Fautin, Daphne and Gerald Allen. *Field Guide to Anemonefishes and Their Host Sea Anemones.* Perth, Australia: Western Australian Museum, 1986.

Goldstein, Robert J. *Marine Reef Aquarium Handbook.* Hauppauge, NY: Barron's Educational Series, Inc., 1997.

Haywood, Martyn, and Sue Wells. *The Manual of Marine Invertebrates.* Morris Plains, NJ: Tetra Press, 1989.

Heslinga, G., T. C. Watson, and T. Isama. *Giant Clam Farming.* Honolulu, HI: Pacific Fisheries Development Foundation (NMFS/NOAA), 1990.

Holliday, Les. *Coral Reefs.* Morris Plains, NJ: Salamander Books, 1989.

Hoover, John P. *Hawaii's Fishes.* Honolulu, HI: Mutual Publishing Company, 1993.

Humann, Paul. *Reef Fish Identification.* Jacksonville, FL: New World Publications, 1990.

James, Barry. *A Fishkeeper's Guide to Aquarium Plants*. New York: Salamander Books, 1986.

Kaplan, E. H. *A Field Guide to Coral Reefs of the Caribbean and Florida*. Boston, MA: Houghton-Mifflin Company, 1982.

_____. *A Field Guide to Southeastern and Caribbean Seashores*. Boston, MA: Houghton-Mifflin Company, 1988.

Knop, Daniel. *Giant Clams*. Ettlingen, Germany: Dahne-Verlag, 1996.

Littler, Diane S., Mark M. Littler, Katina E. Bucher, and James N. Norris. *Marine Plants of the Caribbean—A Field Guide from Florida to Brazil*. Washington, DC: Smithsonian Institution Press, 1989.

Magruder, William H. and Jeffrey W. Hunt. *Seaweeds of Hawaii*. Honolulu, HI: Oriental Publishing Company, 1979.

Margulis, L. and K.V. Schwartz. *Five Kingdoms*. San Francisco, CA: W.H. Freeman and Co., 1982.

Michael, Scott W. *Reef Fishes. Volume 1*. Shelburne, VT: Microcosm, 1998.

Moe, Martin A., Jr. *The Marine Aquarium Reference. Systems and Invertebrates*. Plantation, FL: Green Turtle Publications, 1989.

Morris, Percy A. *A Field Guide to Shells*. Boston, MA: Houghton-Mifflin Company, 1973.

Myers, Robert F. *Micronesian Reef Fishes*. Guam: Coral Graphics, 1989.

Paletta, Michael S. *The New Marine Aquarium*. Shelburne, VT: Microcosm, 1999.

Rataj, Karel and Thomas J. Horeman. *Aquarium Plants*. Neptune, NJ: TFH Publications, Inc., 1977.

Riehl, R. and H. A. Baensch. *Aquarium Atlas. Volume 1*. English edition. Shelburne, VT: Microcosm, 1997.

_____. *Aquarium Atlas. Volume 3*. English edition. Shelburne, VT: Microcosm, 1997.

Roessler, Carl. *The Underwater Wilderness. Life Around the Great Reefs.* New York: McGraw-Hill, 1986.

Scheurmann, Ines. *The New Aquarium Handbook.* Hauppauge, NY: Barron's Educational Series, Inc., 1985.

Smith, Deboyd L. *A Guide to Marine Coastal Plankton and Marine Invertebrate Larvae.* Dubuque, IA: Kendall-Hunt Publishing Company, 1977.

Spotte, Stephen. *Seawater Aquariums.* New York: John Wiley & Sons, 1979.

_____. *Captive Seawater Fishes.* New York: John Wiley & Sons, New York, 1992.

Sprung, Julian and Charles Delbeek. *The Reef Aquarium, Volume II.* Coconut Grove, FL: Ricordea Publishing, 1997.

Stawikowski, Rainer. *The Biotope Aquarium.* Neptune, NJ: TFH Publications, Inc., 1993.

Steene, Roger C. *Coral Reefs: Nature's Richest Realm.* Bathurst, NSW, Australia: Crawford House Press, 1990.

Sterba, Gunter. *The Aquarium Encyclopedia.* Cambridge, MA: MIT Press, 1983.

Stodola, Jiri. *The Encyclopedia of Water Plants.* Neptune, NJ: TFH Publications, Inc., 1967.

Taylor, W. Randolph. *Marine Algae of the Tropical and Subtropical Coasts of the Americas.* Ann Arbor, MI: University of Michigan Press, 1960.

Tullock, John. *Successful Saltwater Aquariums.* Harbor City, CA: Coralife, 1994.

_____. *The Reef Tank Owner's Manual. 3rd ed.* Harbor City, CA: Coralife, 1996.

_____. *Natural Reef Aquariums.* Shelburne, VT: Microcosm, 1997.

_____. *Your First Marine Aquarium.* Hauppauge, NY: Barron's Educational Series, Inc., 1998.

_____. *Clownfish and Sea Anemones.* Hauppauge, NY: Barron's Educational Series, Inc., 1998.

Veron, J. E. N. *Corals of Australia and the Indo-Pacific.* North Ryde, NSW, Australia: Angus and Robertson, 1986.

_____. *Corals in Space and Time. The Biogeography and Evolution of the Scleractinia.* Sydney, NSW, Australia: UNSW Press, 1995.

Walls, J. G., ed. *Encyclopedia of Marine Invertebrates.* Neptune, NJ: TFH Publications, Inc., 1982.

Wilkens, P. and J. Birkholz. *Invertebrates- Tube-, Soft-, and Branching Corals.* Wuppertal, Germany: Englebert Pfriem Verlag, 1986.

Wilkerson, Joyce D. *Clownfishes.* Shelburne, VT: Microcosm, 1998.

Wood, Elizabeth. *Corals of the World.* Neptune, NJ: TFH Publications, Inc., 1983.

Zann, Leon P. *Marine Community Aquarium.* Neptune, NJ: TFH Publications, Inc., 1988.